Cultural Relations
and U.S. Foreign Policy

CHARLES A. THOMSON
& WALTER H. C. LAVES

Cultural Relations
and U.S. Foreign Policy

Indiana University Press
BLOOMINGTON

To
Herman B Wells
whose educational pioneering has enriched
the cultural life of Indiana, the United
States, and the world community

Preface

UPON THE COMPLETION of our joint volume, *Unesco: Purpose, Progress, Prospects* in 1957, it was Charles Thomson's hope that we might jointly undertake a major work on the role of cultural relations in United States foreign policy. He saw such a study as an opportunity to synthesize his thinking and experience of a quarter of a century of service with the United States government. He had been an active participant in the development of policy and program and was convinced of the importance of cultural activities in the conduct of United States foreign relations. Generous grants from the Eli Lilly Endowment and from Indiana University made it possible for the project to be undertaken and completed.

Charles Thomson's sudden death in 1961 meant much more to the future of our joint effort than the inevitable delay in publication. It removed the possibility of achieving the kind of integrated thinking and writing that had typified preparation of the Unesco volume. While we had worked jointly on the outline and on some parts of the manuscript, he had conducted the historical research in Bloomington while I was temporarily engaged in Washington in a closely related study for the U.S. Advisory Commission on Educational Exchanges. I had also undertaken extensive interviews in Asia, the Middle East, and Europe before my Washington assignment. The task of achieving a joint product in which he was to be the senior author was to have begun the week that followed his death.

The historical section, Part One, was essentially Charles Thomson's creation. Most of his writing has been preserved, though some gaps had to be filled in where his manuscript was incomplete. The content of Part Two had been discussed in general terms over a period of many years of our association and during the intensive planning of the book. Many of the issues had been the subject of joint consultation with a variety of specialists and with officials of various governments. None of these chapters, however, had the benefit of Charles Thomson's scrutiny. They would have gained much from his wisdom and conscientious attention.

Although the project lost its senior author, it gained a full collaborator in my wife, who from the start had been involved in discussions of the manuscript. I owe her much more than the usual felicitous phrases about a husband's appreciation of tolerant understanding during the painful maturation of a book. She became in fact a co-author and shares in whatever merit may be found in the finished product. For its shortcomings or errors I take full personal responsibility.

Many persons have contributed both directly and indirectly to the completion of this study. To attempt to list them would introduce the usual risks of omission, which in this case are seriously augmented by the absence of one of the authors. Special thanks should go to Francis J. Colligan of the Department of State, who through his central involvement over many years in this aspect of U.S. foreign relations was able to give much wise counsel; to Alice Siminsky, who assisted Charles Thomson throughout the early stages of the manuscript; to Bonnie Van Orman for secretarial support; and to Miriam S. Farley of the Indiana University Press for editorial counsel.

WALTER H. C. LAVES

Contents

Abbreviations

AEO	Atomic Energy Organization
AID	Agency for International Development
CIAA	Coordinator of Inter-American Affairs
CIER	Commission for International Educational Reconstruction
COA	Commission on the Occupied Areas
ECA	Economic Cooperation Administration
FAO	Food and Agricultural Organization
FOA	Foreign Operations Administration
GARIOA	Government and Relief in Occupied Areas
HICOG	Office of the United States High Commissioner for Germany
ICA	International Cooperation Administration
IES	International Educational Exchange Service
IIA	International Information Administration
ILO	International Labor Organization
IMG	International Media Guarantee
ITU	International Telecommunications Union
MSA	Mutual Security Agency

11

NASA	National Aeronautics and Space Agency
NATO	North Atlantic Treaty Organization
OCE	Office of Cultural Exchange
OECD	Organization for Economic Cooperation and Development
OEE	Office of Educational Exchange
OIC	Office of International Information and Cultural Affairs
OMGUS	Office of Military Government of the United States for Germany
OWI	Office of War Information
SCAP	Supreme Commander for the Allied Powers
TCA	Technical Cooperation Administration
Unesco	United Nations Educational, Scientific and Cultural Organization
Unicef	United Nations Children's Emergency Fund
UPU	Universal Postal Union
USIA	United States Information Agency
USIS	United States Information Service
WHO	World Health Organization
WMO	World Meteorological Organization
WPA	Works Progress Administration

Introduction

ONE

The Purpose of this Book

THIS BOOK DEALS with a new and rapidly growing dimension in the conduct of United States foreign relations. In less than 25 years, the American government has become involved in a broad range of cultural activities including educational exchanges, information programs, and technical assistance. A quick glance around the world will reveal the variety and extent of our government's operations in these fields.

In Cairo, the USIS librarian opens the doors of the library and finds waiting a journalist, five students from the technical college and the University of Cairo, four prospective exchange students due to go to the United States in another month for a year's study, a young doctor, an engineer, and an official of the Ministry of Education. Inside, the tables and chairs have already been arranged since the doors closed last night. *Life, Look*, the *National Geographic Magazine*, the *American Political Science Review*, the *American Historical Review*, and many other popular and professional journals as well as the *New York Times* and the *New York Herald-Tribune* are ready to be taken again from the shelves. The books are all in order and the catalog cards are as neatly tucked away in their alphabetically labeled drawers as they are in the public library of Danville, Illinois, or Tampa, Florida. All day, while the dry heat blows in from the desert and the palm trees rustle in the adjoining garden, more people—men,

15

women, boys, and girls—come and go. Some remain to read at the big round tables, others return or withdraw books. Many pause to look at the bulletin board, on which are posted notices of documentary film showings, of English-language classes, of coming theatrical and musical performances.

The Cairo library is one of 176 information libraries maintained by the U.S. government in 80 or more countries around the world. In the course of one year (1960–61) the Cairo library, with total holdings of 31,000 books, recorded 163,948 visitors and a total book circulation in excess of 62,000. The 176 libraries reported more than 28 million visitors, holdings of 2.5 million books, 31,309 subscriptions to periodicals, and a circulation of 8 million—roughly the equivalent of the annual circulation of books in the New York City Public Library.

March 9, 1962, will be remembered by most Americans as the day they spent glued to their television or radio sets, following the dramatic space flight of Colonel John Glenn. On the same day millions of people in nearly every country of the world were participating in the event with the help of world-wide mass media coverage arranged by the USIA.[1] By means of radio, television, film, and wireless news services the USIA was helping these people to see and hear what was happening.

Weeks in advance "Focus Infinity," a filmed television show, was distributed in many languages through 67 USIA posts abroad, so that it could be run on the day of the flight. An estimated 125 million people saw this film. Footage of the actual flight was air expressed to 17 countries that did not get normal commercial service. USIS television programs in Japan showed the film to an estimated 20 million, and the USIS Latin American program showed it to a probable 12 million in 18 countries. Press background stories had been sent in advance, again in several languages and accompanied by pictures. By teletype the actual flight was reported while it was in progress. Twenty-two USIA stations in Latin America, 17 in Africa, 17 in the Near East, 22 in Europe, and 15 in the Far East received this service for immediate transmission to the local press. To cover the flight story USIA sent out 23,000 photographs, 75 color transparencies, and columns of comment and analysis. The Mexico City plant of USIA

produced 30,000 copies of a pamphlet in Spanish and Portuguese for
Latin America. Within a few days 83,000 pamphlets produced in
the Lebanon plant were being distributed in Arabic, Turkish, and
French throughout the Middle East. Special stories on the Nigerian
and Zanzibar tracking stations were featured in Africa. The USIA
official magazine *Amerika* in Russian, its Polish-language edition, and
Al Hayat, the U.S. Arabic magazine, all carried special features on
Glenn. The Voice of America was on the air for nine consecutive
hours of broadcasting about the flight, so that millions of listeners
abroad could follow the details in 37 different languages including
mandarin Chinese, Armenian, and Russian.

Within 72 hours film sequences were on their way to 30 countries, newsreel sequences with Spanish sound tracks went to 18
countries in Latin America, and others in Arabic, French, and English went to 30 countries in Africa. A monthly newsreel produced by
USIA, *Today*, displayed the Glenn flight in 700 motion picture
houses throughout Africa. There followed a documentary film, re-
produced in 1,500 separate prints, that went to 106 countries with
narration in 32 languages. It was shown in Japan, Yugoslavia, Egypt,
and many other countries. While the flight was in progress, U.S. Information Centers around the world had on display special exhibits
prepared for the purpose by NASA.

This was but one of many kinds of activities carried on by the
United States for the purpose of informing people of other countries about the American people and the policies of our government.
The program includes news and feature stories for radio, press, motion pictures, and television, made available in nearly every country
of the world. The Voice of America sends over 700 hours weekly of
broadcasts in 38 languages. The USIA maintains a staff of over 1,250
offices in more than 100 countries.

A distinguished political leader of a Middle Eastern country has
just completed a six-week visit to the United States upon the invitation of the Department of State. He has previously held high political offices in his own country and still exerts so much influence that
it is probable he will one day again be a principal official of the
government.

He was invited under the so-called leaders program and was accompanied by his wife. Arrangements for the tour through the United States were made by the Governmental Affairs Institute, a nongovernmental organization engaged in research and public affairs activities. This is one of several private agencies that are under contract with the Department of State to look after distinguished official visitors under the leader program. The six-week tour was planned in detail before our guest's arrival, after correspondence with him before he left home. Some minor adjustments were made after his arrival to accommodate his special interests.

Because of his academic background and his concern with the educational development of his people, Mr. X visited several major universities, including Columbia, Harvard, Cornell, Indiana, Wisconsin, and California. At each he was the guest of faculty and of foreign students from his own country. He gave a public lecture at each institution and participated in informal seminars on recent political developments in his country—developments that are of vital significance to the United States. On each campus he visited the libraries and principal research centers to become acquainted with American educational developments and to explore resources pertinent to the educational tasks at home.

The tour, at his request, included leisurely visits to the Grand Canyon, Niagara Falls, and Williamsburg. Interviews and sightseeing were arranged at the Ford Motor Company in Detroit and Disneyland in Los Angeles as well as places of interest in New York, Chicago, and San Francisco. In New York and Washington discussion conferences were arranged with foreign trade and industrial leaders and government officials especially interested in his country. He spent some time at the United Nations headquarters, which he had never seen, though his country has long been a member. He participated in five television and radio interview programs at different points on the trip. Wherever feasible, luncheons, dinners, and informal receptions were arranged in private homes to bring the visitors into closer contact with American life. In a few places conveniently located for this purpose there were visits to farms and rural homes. It is estimated that these guests were in direct contact with at least 3,000 individual Americans.

In 1961 the Department of State brought nearly 800 such visitors to the United States under the leader program. For each of these, tours were arranged corresponding to their special interests, which have included industry, finance, journalism, economic development, music, business, politics, and local government.

Each year since 1950, 20 to 25 outstanding journalists from 15 or more foreign countries have come to this country for a period of four months to work, study, and travel. The purpose of the program is to help them to understand the United States and to interpret news of this country accurately to their readers. They come as guests of the U.S. government and engage in a carefully prepared program managed by the Department of Journalism at Indiana University. Intensive seminars on journalism and on many aspects of American society —law, government, economics, foreign policy, sociology—arranged at the University are followed by travel and by further study in selected cities, then by internship assignments with American newspapers covering about one month. The project gives each participant an opportunity to see American democracy in practice at national, state, and local levels and the workings of the American press. The composition of the group each year is multinational and has included journalists from every part of the world. Newspapers, radio stations, television stations, advertising agencies, public relations agencies, and printing houses from coast to coast have cooperated in the project each year.[2]

During the school year 1961–62 the children of Pine Valley Central School, South Dayton, New York, traded home economics teachers with the South Oxford Domestic Science Centre of Oxfordshire, England. Buckeye Union High School of Buckeye, Arizona, traded an English teacher for a teacher from the Technical Industrial Institute of Naples, Italy. Carritos College, Norwalk, California, exchanged a mathematics and science teacher for one from Taroona, Tasmania, Australia. Public School No. 30, Thomas Carr Howe School, and George Washington High School, all of Indianapolis, Indiana, exchanged with schools in, respectively, Cheshire, England, King Edward VI School of Southampton, and Fishguard Secondary School of Pembrokeshire, Wales; Casady School of Oklahoma City exchanged with Theodor Mommsenschule, Bad Oldesloe, Holstein, Germany.

In all there were nearly 200 such direct exchanges of teachers; all were made possible by grants from the U.S. government. In addition, without direct exchange arrangements, some 250 American teachers went abroad to teach or study and about 50 teachers from foreign countries came to the United States to teach—all under U.S. government grants.

A midwestern university professor of social psychology establishes himself and his family, which includes a wife and three children, at a university in a Latin American country. He will be there for a year, carrying on research in the field of his specialization and also offering occasional lectures to groups of advanced students. He will be asked to consult with other members of the faculty about ways of developing institutions and research in social psychology and library resources necessary to both. His family will live as members of the academic community, his children attending school and acquiring, more quickly no doubt than their parents, conversational competence in the local language.

Out of this experience, Professor X will develop materials for articles in professional journals in the United States and will collect new data for teaching a course at his home university on comparative aspects of social psychology. There will be opportunity for him to visit other Latin American universities on his way home, and perhaps to attend a regional conference in his professional field. His wife, if all goes well, will become an active member of the university community abroad, learning new ways and contributing to a better understanding of the American way of life. Their children will mingle freely, as children so easily do, with native and other foreign children, and will thus become a part of a small but genuine international community that can provide insights and understandings of value throughout their lives. This experience may bear fruit for the children in various ways: in language proficiency; in a vocational bent toward such fields as international trade or the foreign service; in an interest in foreign cultures and cultural anthropology; or simply in a heightened awareness of the kind of complex and varied world in which they live.

This is a generalized but not inaccurate sketch of what has happened to hundreds of American participants in the Fulbright program, which in 1961–62 took 1,942 American scholars, teachers, and students abroad and brought to the United States 4,861 foreigners.[3]

A College for Teacher Training is today in full swing in Bangkok, Thailand, staffed by Thai faculty members, most of whom have received advanced academic degrees from American universities as participants under a U.S. technical assistance program. This college, well equipped with 380 teachers, a library of 73,700 books and periodicals, and a first-class physical plant, has an enrollment of 4,900 and trains teachers for elementary and secondary schools throughout Thailand. The college was developed through a cooperative arrangement between the U.S. and the Thai governments, and received its primary assistance in the United States from Indiana University.

The development of institutions of higher learning has been a major objective of the U.S. technical assistance program. Today assistance for this purpose is being provided to more than 26 countries of Asia, Africa, and Latin America. The developmental stage of all these projects has involved the sending of large numbers of participants to the United States for training as teachers and administrators, and of many American teachers to provide interim instruction and counsel while the participants were in training.

In most underdeveloped countries American technicians may be seen at work today providing assistance in such fields as irrigation, engineering, public finance, poultry farming, soil conservation, soil improvement, malaria control, and public sanitation—all a part of the U.S. technical assistance effort. In the fiscal year July 1961—June 1962 these technicians were estimated to total 4,951. At the same time 11,953 participants from 83 underdeveloped countries were receiving technical training in the United States.

English-language classes are being conducted by the American government in more than 50 countries with an estimated attendance of well over a quarter of a million persons. Classes are attended by high government officials in some countries, especially in Africa, and everywhere the classes include youth, business and professional men, and a wide range of civil service personnel. In addition, the U.S. government has organized seminars for more than 5,000 teachers of English to help them provide better instruction.

In Gondar, Ethiopia, the Public Health Training College, financed jointly by the Ethiopian government, the United States AID, the World Health Organization, and Unicef is staffed today by 57 Ethiopians and 15 foreigners. It has graduated 230 rural health workers, trained in curative and preventive medicine, nursing, or sanitation. Before its creation in 1954 there was no health training of this kind in all of Ethiopia.

The United States assists health programs in more than 40 countries and through AID alone employs approximately 300 technical personnel. Extensive medical training assistance also takes place in many countries through the U.S. Public Health Service, foundations, and many other nongovernmental groups.[4]

In 1962 the United States joined with 85 other countries of the United Nations and its specialized agencies in financing technical assistance through a total of 3,657 experts sent to 40 countries and territories of Africa; 29 countries and territories of the Americas; 29 countries and territories of Asia and the Far East; 18 countries of Europe; and 13 countries and territories of the Middle East.

United States contributions assisted in the financing of U.N. fellowship awards to 1,235 nationals of 40 African countries and territories; to 1,061 nationals of 29 countries and territories of the Americas; to 1,099 nationals of 37 Asian and Far Eastern countries and territories; to 652 nationals of 13 countries and territories of the Middle East; and to 1,384 nationals of 32 countries of Europe.

The subjects of expert assistance and of fellowship studies ranged across the fields of public health, sanitation, medicine, education, mass communication, industrial development, meteorology, community development, labor conditions, agriculture, fisheries, forestry, civil aviation, atomic energy development, and telecommunications.[5]

The U.S. government today also carries on abroad a variety of other cultural activities as an accepted part of its conduct of foreign relations. It helps to finance and arrange performances abroad by

American orchestras, glee clubs, soloists, and theater companies. It helps support programs of Unesco and the other specialized agencies of the United Nations, as well as the central United Nations technical assistance activities. It helps finance a new East-West educational and cultural center in Hawaii. It sends American specialists to participate in major international educational conferences such as that in Addis Abbaba in 1962 for planning the educational development of Africa. It provides major financial assistance for American scholars, research workers, and teachers to go abroad and for foreigners to come to the United States. It promotes U.S. participation in trade fairs in the U.S.S.R. and other countries. It helped scientists of the world to organize and finance the International Geophysical Year and has helped make it possible for a group of outstanding historians to participate in the writing of a scientific and cultural history of mankind.

This wide range of activities is but a small part of the total involvement of the American people in transnational cultural relations. Immigrants and emigrants, traders and investors, missionaries, scholars, and tourists all have been carriers of knowledge and ideas. Educational and religious institutions, foundations, mass media, commercial enterprises, and individual initiative have helped weave a network of relationships that is the foundation upon which government activities have been built. For all of the nineteenth century and for much of the twentieth cultural cooperation was without governmental direction, though government often facilitated individual efforts through such means as treaties of friendship or immigration and emigration policies.

Not until the 1930s did the government of the United States begin to give more systematic attention to such cultural exchanges, and in 1938 it launched its first formal program of cultural relations—a program to stimulate, encourage, and channel cultural activities in line with foreign policy. From that date to the present the federal government has allocated increasing funds to its participation in cultural activities, and it has increasingly sought to direct the cultural activities in which it takes part more precisely to the attainment of foreign policy objectives. But even now, it must be remembered, governmental activities do not predominate.

Government involvement was to be broadened and deepened beyond anyone's expectations during the 1950s with the general deterioration of international relations and the mounting tension between the free world and the Communist countries. Today, with the decline of war as a practicable method in the conduct of international affairs, transnational cultural relations have become one of the two areas in which the necessary peaceful competition with the Communist countries can be pursued. But these two areas—the economic and the cultural—are also those in which the free world countries need to cooperate with each other and with the newly developing countries. Among themselves, the free world nations will find cultural cooperation basic to the developing and strengthening of their own institutions of freedom. In relation to the newly developing countries, the free world will find cultural cooperation an essential means for achieving a sense of common purpose in a world community.

The effectiveness with which cooperation in the realm of education, science, the arts, and technology is carried on within the free world, with the newly developing countries, and with the Communist world can profoundly influence the prospects for the survival of non-Communist countries and for the attainment of conditions for peaceful, though competitive, coexistence with the Communist world. It will determine, to a considerable extent, the prospects for attaining the basic objectives of American foreign policy.

This books seeks to describe how the American government became involved in transnational cultural action; to explain how such action can contribute to the attainment of our major objectives in foreign policy; and to outline the requirements for an effective governmental program.

PART I

The Evolution
of Cultural Programs

TWO

The Beginnings: 1938-1945

Two SMALL STEPS in 1938 marked the first moves toward assignment of government funds and personnel for a continuing program of cultural relations. In May the Interdepartmental Committee on Cooperation with the American Republics—linking together thirteen government agencies—met for the first time, with Under Secretary of State Sumner Welles as chairman. In July a new major unit was created in the Department of State—the Division of Cultural Relations. The Committee received for its first year of operations $370,500, the Division $28,000.

But like the grain of mustard seed in the parable, these small beginnings held large ideas. The Committee was concerned with certain aspects of what later came to be called technical cooperation. The Division had to do with the contribution of education, science, and the arts to foreign relations, and the enlistment of government and private agencies in a cooperative effort to this end. During the ensuing two decades or more these ideas expanded in a way never foreseen by their early propagators.

The two steps taken in 1938 were the outgrowth of a series of recommendations and resolutions in which successive Pan American Conferences had called for closer cooperation and interchange in education, science, and the arts.[1] Most recent and most prominent among these had been the approval by the Inter-American Conference for the Maintenance of Peace at Buenos Aires in Decem-

27

ber, 1936, of the Convention for the Promotion of Inter-American
Cultural Relations, providing for the use of government funds for
the exchange of graduate students, teachers, and professors among
the 21 American republics. The Convention had been drafted in the
Department of State with the assistance of a number of advisers from
private life, and was sponsored at Buenos Aires by the United States
delegation. It was the view of the delegation that the promotion of
cultural relations was "one of the most practical means of developing in the American republics a public opinion which would favor
and support a rule of peace throughout the Western Hemisphere."[2]

TRANSNATIONAL CULTURAL ACTIVITIES BEFORE 1938

Until 1938 the United States government had left the responsibility for transnational cultural activities in private hands. Domesti-
cally, the support of education had rested with the states, local governments, and private groups, and that of the arts primarily with
philanthropists. In science the federal government had played a more
active although a far from prominent role. Agencies such as the Departments of Agriculture, Commerce, and Interior had carried on research in their own laboratories, and federal funds for agricultural
research had been given to land-grant colleges and experiment stations. But in general, within our own frontiers the responsibility of
the federal government for activities relating to education, science,
and the arts had been minimal.

Correlatively, it had assumed no responsibility for transnational
activities in these fields. The government had taken no defined attitude beyond that of general, if casual, encouragement of cultural activities as a phase of peaceful cooperation among peoples. Like trade,
cultural activities were viewed as predominantly private in character,
though they could be helped or hindered by government action; essentially reciprocal and mutually advantageous; directed toward nongovernmental ends but presumably consistent with the objectives of
foreign policy.

But even less than trade did they enjoy any consistent participation or support from government. What government did was largely
casual and sporadic. Some outstanding intellectual figures had served

as diplomatic representatives abroad—not only such statesmen-writers as Benjamin Franklin and Thomas Jefferson, who first published his *Notes on Virginia* in Paris, but such later literary men as Washington Irving, Nathaniel Hawthorne, William Dean Howells, James Russell Lowell, and the historians George Bancroft and John Lothrop Motley.

In 1840 what might be called the first continuing activity in official cultural relations originated in a joint resolution of the Congress, providing for exchange of published materials between the Library of Congress and foreign libraries. In 1867 the Smithsonian Institution was assigned responsibility for interchange of public documents with institutions abroad. In 1868 the first annual report of the United States Commissioner of Education carried information on education in other countries; and beginning in 1892 his office was charged with the task of making and issuing studies of education abroad.[3] In 1892 the National Bureau of Standards was authorized to receive as guests foreign scientists and technicians.

Some single actions were of more dramatic significance. In 1900 almost 1,300 Cuban teachers were brought to the United States on army transports for courses in English and other subjects during a six-week summer session at Harvard University.[4] But the most striking initiative was related to the Boxer indemnity. President Theodore Roosevelt proposed in December, 1907, to return to China that part of the Boxer indemnity fund which exceeded the sum of actual damage and injury. As a result, by the authority of joint resolutions of the Congress in 1908 and 1924, more than $18 million was remitted to China to be used for educational purposes. The Chinese government placed the funds in a trust for the education of Chinese young people in China and in the United States, for research, and for such other educational purposes as the establishment of libraries and museums. In consequence more than 2,000 Chinese men and women were trained in American colleges and universities, and they returned to their homeland to take places of increasing leadership in public and private life.[5]

During the first four decades of the twentieth century the United States took part in a number of Pan-American Congresses concerned with education, science, and social welfare. It contributed small sums to the cultural activities of the Pan American Union and a few specialized inter-American organizations, and not exceeding $9,000 annually to the International Council of Scientific Unions. In the course of World War I the Creel Committee on Public Information focused on publicizing the objectives and activities of the American war effort, but gave practically no attention to the cultural field. One exception was the establishment in seven Mexican cities of American reading rooms, and the provision of classes in English, French, shorthand, and bookkeeping which were reported to have enrolled 30,000 students.[6] But no clear, continuous, and consistent policy underlay these diverse and scattered ventures.

Meanwhile, private activities had created a far-reaching web of relationships between the American people and other peoples. Education in the United States, from the colonial period to the end of the nineteenth century, had been largely shaped by influences imported from such countries as England, Holland, France, and Germany. But in the early decades of the twentieth century this country began to export influence, as a result of the writings of John Dewey and other educators, and of a growing desire in many nations to learn of America's democratic system of public schools for all, its widespread experimentation in curriculum and methods of instruction, and the extension of scientific research to all aspects of the educational process. For decades American students had gone abroad for advanced work in medicine, science, and numerous other scholarly fields, and in art and music. This movement continued after 1900, but it was progressively balanced by a counter-movement which by the late thirties had brought nine or ten thousand foreign students to work in American colleges and universities.

Scientists and other scholars in the United States were linked to their colleagues abroad through periodic congresses, a network of associations, and journals of international circulation. In the arts, the interaction of American and foreign influences was more evident perhaps in literature, but was by no means negligible in music, architecture, and the visual arts; and American jazz had won a world-wide following. Contacts in most of the above fields were stimulated and amplified by the efforts of philanthropic foundations.

More widely, the American missionary enterprise had carried many phases of the American way of life as well as religious ideas to Asia and Africa. American business through trade and investment was exerting an expanding influence on cultural relations as well as on economic life. The international movement of books and publications was accelerating. The study and use of the English language were everywhere gaining ground.

Wider still, perhaps, was the impact of the flood of American tourists abroad, the tide of communications between immigrants who had settled in the United States and their relatives and friends remaining at home, the information purveyed by news agencies, and the world-wide circulation of American motion pictures with their pervasive, if at times distorted, images of life in the United States.

Thus when the United States government began formal and continuing participation in transnational cultural activities, there existed a vast and varied private network of cultural relations and influences between the United States and other countries, primarily but not exclusively those of Europe. This book is primarily devoted to the role of government in cultural relations, but it should never be forgotten that the role of private agencies and individuals is far broader than that of government.

WHY DID GOVERNMENT EMBARK ON CULTURAL RELATIONS?

The United States was the last of the major powers to develop a government program in the cultural field. The French had initiated such activities during the second half of the nineteenth century. Between the two wars Germany, Italy, and Japan, as well as the Soviet Union, gave increasing attention to this phase of international relations. Great Britain set up the British Council in 1934.[7]

Why, it may be asked, did governments in this period invade a field they had previously left to private hands? The answer is to be found largely in the advance of science, democracy, and education which had accompanied the Industrial Revolution. Science and technology had accelerated the development of modern means of communication. Telegraph, cable, and radio, the motion picture and the modern printing press, all facilitated a more rapid and more extensive flow of news and information across frontiers.[8] The corresponding acceleration of travel by railway, steamer, automobile, and airplane increased the number of face-to-face meetings. These augmented not only the flow of information, but also slower and deeper currents of communication, such as the movement of students, teachers, and scholars.

Second, the extension of political democracy had enhanced the importance of "common people" everywhere. Their support of foreign policy was increasingly cultivated by their own governments, and their favor and understanding were increasingly courted by other governments. Foreign policy was no longer the privileged preserve of professional diplomats. Correlatively, the rapid growth of international economic ties forged by investment and trade, together with improvements in communication, had made the common man more conscious of what went on in other countries. His job, his income, his individual security might be shattered by the outbreak of armed conflict or a market crash in a distant area of the world. Events abroad affected a larger public than ever before.

Finally, the spread of popular education had endowed this larger public with new knowledge. Its horizon of interest was not necessarily limited to the neighborhood, the local community, or even the nation. Education was a tool whose use led to a better life and to a wider world. Citizenship demanded more active participation on many new fronts. The voice of the people was increasingly heard in the formulation of foreign policy. Thus the growing importance of the new public, its new knowledge and power, joined to the stepped-up facilities for international communication, led to the demand that peoples should speak to peoples. This demand was reflected in the adoption by governments of programs to reach the minds and hearts of other peoples.

Particularly for the United States, certain additional factors may be mentioned. During the first half of the twentieth century it became first a world power, and then one of the two dominant nations on the international scene. Power inevitably attracts attention, not only to the military, political, and economic strength of a people, but also to its cultural life. Simultaneously, the United States shifted from the position of a cultural colony to that of a cultural metropolis. Instead of looking as formerly to the older centers of Europe for models in dress and fashion, in science and art, in literature and the stage, it developed a growing pride and confidence in its own creativity and leadership. No longer merely an importer of culture, it became an exporter as well. Finally, the threat to freedom and democracy of aggressive Nazism and later of Soviet Communism called for closer cultural bonds, as well as political alliances and economic alignments, with the opponents of these strategists of international tyranny. In the face of such a challenge, the task of reaching other people seemed too big and too closely related to the interests of foreign policy for private effort to carry alone.

WHY START IN LATIN AMERICA?

While the cultural relations activities initiated in 1938 were ultimately to become world-wide in scope, their immediate focus was on Latin America. Why was this so? Although the ominous course of world events in the 1930s had underlined the importance of the Latin American republics to the security and welfare of the United States, these countries had largely been passed over, since preference in the cultural exchanges developed by colleges, universities, foundations, and other private agencies was given first to Europe and then to certain countries of Asia. Notable exceptions to this trend were the work of the International Health Board of the Rockefeller Foundation in Latin America and the support granted by the Carnegie Endowment for International Peace to inter-American exchanges of professors, students, and books.

With the first Conference of American States in 1889 the United States had begun an effort to foster a cooperative inter-American system. Commerce increased and communications improved. But toward the end of the nineteenth century came dreams of United States political expansion and the spread of economic imperialism. In the early years of the twentieth century our relations with Latin America were strained by Theodore Roosevelt's action in Panama, later pithily summarized in the phrase, "I took the Canal Zone"; by a series of armed interventions in the Caribbean area; by Theodore Roosevelt's tutelary interpretation of the Monroe Doctrine, which sought to justify such interventions by attributing a regional police power to the United States; and later by Woodrow Wilson's nonrecognition policy.

A counter-trend was initiated under Presidents Harding, Coolidge, and Hoover, with the progressive liquidation of various armed interventions, and the mission of Ambassador Dwight Morrow in Mexico. In 1930 the Department of State issued the Clark Memorandum on the Monroe Doctrine retracting the Roosevelt interpretation. This new trend was carried forward by President Franklin D. Roosevelt in 1933 under the Good Neighbor policy.

Before the distrust aroused by the "awkward imperialism" of the United States, the peoples of the two Americas remained largely unknown and indifferent to each other. In contrast with the currents of cultural interchange between the Latin American countries and the leading nations of Europe—Germany, Great Britain, Italy, and especially France, as well as the motherlands, Spain and Portugal—the ignorance of the other American republics about the United States was exceeded only by that of the latter about its neighbors to the south.

In most of the Latin American republics at this period French was the second language (after Spanish or Portuguese), and German was widely studied. Comparatively few students from the republics to the south were in the colleges and universities of the United States, while almost no students from this country were taking courses in Latin American institutions. The book trade in South America was principally in the hands of the English, French, Germans, Italians, and Spaniards. Relatively few books or magazines from the United States were on sale. If an American book were wanted, it had usually to be ordered direct from the publishers, an irksome and sometimes fruitless effort.[9]

While in subsequent years the inter-American exchange of students and professors increased (during the 1930s approximately one thousand Latin American students were annually enrolled in American colleges and universities), and the study of Spanish and courses on Latin American subjects multiplied in the institutions of the United States, there were still outstanding deficiencies. When in 1938 the Director of the National Library at Bogotá, Colombia, was appointed to his country's legation at Washington, he tried to find in his library a history of the United States in Spanish. The only volume available referred to the seventeenth century. In fact, throughout all Latin America, no good one-volume history of the United States existed in Spanish or Portuguese. Reciprocally, although our achievements in historical research on Latin America were considerable there was an almost complete absence in the United States of adequate histories of the individual Latin American republics.

The need for more active cultural interchange with Latin America was dramatized from a strange quarter. "Nothing would be more fitting than a statue of Adolph Hitler in the Pan American Union," was the ironic comment of a Latin American diplomat early in World War II. "Who more than he has been responsible for drawing the American republics closer together?" The Nazi drive during the 1930s to win the favor of the countries of South and Central America, allied with similar efforts by the Italians and Japanese, threatened to undermine the efforts of half a century to transform Pan-Americanism from a pretentious phrase into the substance of solid unity among the republics of the hemisphere. It was interpreted as making a cultural program on the part of the United States an urgent necessity.[10]

The German program had been gathering force for two decades or more. Libraries in Latin America, university as well as public, had on their shelves more German than United States publications. The teaching of German was widely encouraged. Moreover, German scientific, technical, and medical books had been translated into Spanish and Portuguese. Some nine hundred foreign primary and secondary schools had been set up in Latin America, of which three-fourths were German and the rest Italian and Japanese. Professors were loaned to lecture in national universities. Students and technicians received fellowships for study in Germany. Valuable as a base for these and other activities were the numerous groups of emigrant Germans, Italians, and in smaller degree Japanese, who had settled in Brazil, Argentina, Chile, and other republics. Rivalry with the activities of Germany, Italy, and Japan, as well as to some degree with those of France and Great Britain, was a significant motive in the launching of the United States program.

Thus to the people of Latin America the United States seemed distant and alien. At best it appeared indifferent. The current image of the North American was not that of the scholar, the artist, the humanitarian, or even the ordinary, understandable human being. It was in the popular view that of a vigorous people, but rude and crude, avid for money and material goods. Too prevalently it was symbolized by the invading marine with his trampling boots or the exploiting and corrupting capitalist. Such images were made to order for the propaganda of Goebbels. They had to be corrected and humanized if the people of Latin America were to accept the United States as any sort of "good neighbor."

CULTURAL PROGRAMS BEFORE AND DURING WORLD WAR II

The United States began its official cultural program in 1938 by setting up two agencies which, apparently not so much by design as by chance, were complementary in character. As noted earlier, one was the Interdepartmental Committee on Cooperation with the American Republics, the other the Division of Cultural Relations in the Department of State. The first emphasized activities many of which in later years were conducted by the United States as part of "technical cooperation" programs; the second, in its initial stage, the more traditional academic and artistic exchanges that had been the predominant pattern for "intellectual cooperation" under the League of Nations. The first depended on government bodies to carry out its projects; the second looked principally to private organizations.

The Interdepartmental Committee on Cooperation with the American Republics[11] apparently took its origin from a Cabinet discussion in February, 1938, when President Roosevelt voiced the need to discover ways to oppose Axis influence in Latin America. It was established on the oral instructions of the President and was not formally authorized until Public Law 355 came into force on August 9, 1939. This Act was designed to "render closer and more effective the relationship between the American republics" through the services of government agencies "in carrying out the reciprocal undertakings and cooperative purposes" expressed in various actions taken by the Buenos Aires Conference of 1936 and the Lima Conference of 1938. The area of proposed cooperation was broad, including labor, agriculture, communications, public health, public administration, and economic, commercial, and fiscal matters.[12]

The projects of the Interdepartmental Committee came eventually to be classified under three headings: (1) cooperative, scientific and technical projects including agricultural research, experiment stations, and extension activities for the development of rubber and other tropical products such as cacao, cinchona (the source of quinine), drugs, and vegetable fibers; meteorology stations for the international exchange and forecasting of weather information; tidal and magnetic observations; surveys of mineral deposits; promotion of public health; and development of fishery resources; (2) the exchange of specialized information and materials on educational methods and labor standards, and of scientific and technical books and publications, library catalog cards, and albums of folk music; and (3) the "exchange of persons" for education and training in numerous fields such as agriculture, civil aviation, vital statistics, anthropological research, and public administration.

The cooperative projects of the Committee were planned on a bilateral basis, to be of benefit and assistance to both participating governments, and were usually executed jointly. Financial support often came from both parties, but the proportion varied from project to project. While the exchanges of personnel were two-way, they consisted as a rule of the loan of technicians from the United States to the Latin American countries, and the dispatch by those countries of individuals seeking training and experience in the United States largely through in-service activities in agencies of the federal government. Thus the program was cooperative without being precisely reciprocal. A truly reciprocal arrangement is in the nature of the case hardly possible between a country advanced in economic and social development and a less developed country. But the initiative came from the United States.

Cooperating in the Interdepartmental Committee were 25 federal agencies including, in addition to the Department of State, the Departments of Agriculture, Commerce, Labor, and Interior, the Library of Congress, the Public Health Service, and the Smithsonian Institution. From an initial budget of $370,500 in 1940 support steadily expanded, and the Committee was granted approximately $4 million annually for its last three years (1948–50), when a large part of its work was transferred to the Technical Cooperation Administration in the Department of State. The Committee gave to its member agencies a unique opportunity to cooperate in shaping and carrying out abroad activities related to their responsibilities at home.

The Committee worked primarily through short-term technical missions and training grants. This early essay in technical assistance made available the services of many capable specialists, assisted in carrying through hundreds of useful cooperative projects, and developed to some degree friendly relations between the governments of the United States and of the Latin American countries. However, the operation was necessarily a piecemeal one, responding as it did to the individual and often isolated requests of various governments. Its activities were not always focused on the basic needs of the receiving countries, nor were they geared together into an integrated program to advance the economic development of the receiving nations.[13]

The Division of Cultural Relations was responsible for international activities relating to the exchange of professors, teachers, and students; libraries; music, art, and literature; international radio broadcasts; and in general "the dissemination abroad of the representative intellectual and cultural works of the United States and the improvement and broadening of the scope of our cultural relations with other countries."[14] Practically speaking, the most tangible government activity envisaged for the Division at the start was administration for the United States of the Buenos Aires Convention for educational interchange already mentioned.

During this early period, frequent statements emphasized that the program of the Division of Cultural Relations should be reciprocal in character. A group of Congressmen making an official visit to Latin America in 1941 warned against making the cultural program "a one-way road" and declared that equally important with developing among the peoples of the other American republics a better understanding of the way of life of the United States was "knowledge of the many activities being carried on by the Latin-American peoples and governments that will be both educational and inspirational to us as well as valuable to our national life."[15] While, however, a two-way flow of students, professors, and other persons was promoted, the great bulk of the movement consisted of the travel of Latin Americans to the United States. Here again the initiative had come from the United States.

The early thinking concerning the program of the Division of Cultural Relations had primarily related to the intellectual interests of the advantaged classes and had been marked by a certain aristocratic stamp. A plea that the program give greater attention to what later was called technical assistance came in September, 1941, from Vice-President Henry A. Wallace, who had become a member of the General Advisory Committee of the Division of Cultural Relations.[16]

He argued that cultural and economic cooperation were largely inter-dependent, and that cultural activities should be thought of in terms of social functions. He proposed that cultural and economic efforts should be linked in such enterprises as the creation of an inter-American institute for tropical agriculture (later established in Costa Rica), encouragement of the production in tropical areas of crops comple-mentary to those of the United States, and raising the standard of liv-ing through improved agricultural methods. While the Interdepart-mental Committee had from the start viewed economic and cultural cooperation as interdependent, this point of view was new doctrine for many of the members of the General Advisory Committee.

Supplementing the emphasis of the Vice-President but expanding the geographical horizon to Africa, Asia, and Europe, other partici-pants in the discussion pointed out that the people of the world were on the move seeking a better life, better health, better education. In-ternational action would be called for to improve productivity, indus-trial as well as agricultural; nutrition and other aspects of human con-servation; and technological methods and processes to these ends. Economic advance and social welfare, they felt, should become the keynotes of the cultural program of the future.

Correlative to Mr. Wallace's emphasis on economic and social goals was a focus on the middle and lower levels of society in con-trast to the elite. He urged that cultural exchanges should establish helpful relations with these groups, who included 90 per cent of the people of Latin America. Most of them were engaged in agriculture. Without aid to improve their economic lot, thus making it possible for health and education to develop, there would be no solid basis for democracy.[17]

Similarly, members of the Appropriations Committee of the House of Representatives, particularly Congressman Louis C. Rabaut, had stressed that the cultural program should reach "the masses," and not alone "the classes"; the idea of democracy should be carried "not to the caviar class, but to the bread and butter eaters."[18]

In consequence a resolution of the General Advisory Committee as approved at the September, 1941, meeting recognized the need for activities "in all cultural fields, including not only the fine arts, but the fields of public health, agriculture, engineering, industrial engi-neering, and education, together with proposals for financial and commercial action in support of such activity, and more particularly consideration of the techniques and specific training programs involved."[19] The cultural relations program should be planned to help men to acquire skilled trades, to improve agricultural methods, and to forward flood control and irrigation projects. Women should be helped to gain knowledge on how home and family life could be improved through health and sanitation measures, nutrition, and domestic arts.

COOPERATION WITH PRIVATE AGENCIES

In contrast with the emphasis of the Interdepartmental Committee on the use of government agencies and officials, the Division of Cultural Relations was set up primarily to encourage and assist the activities of private organizations in transnational cultural relations. One of the reasons for emphasizing the role of private agencies in the embryonic program was the possible apprehension on their part that the government might seek to dominate or supplant them, or that the introduction of governmental influence in cultural activities abroad might alter for political or economic ends what had been in private hands purely scholarly and intellectual exchange. Second, some opinion held that certain cultural activities might be more palatable and less suspect to foreign peoples if they were handled by private agencies rather than by government. Finally, it was recognized within the government itself that official agencies, even if they would, could not supplant the efforts of private groups, in the sense that the government of a democratic country is only a minor factor in the impact of that country's influence on other nations. Consequently, it was early stressed that "the Department of State has no intention of encroaching upon activities which pertain logically to private initiative. Neither has it any intention of supplanting or diminishing the effective work which is being done by private institutions, but rather to assist them in producing more effective results toward nation-wide coordination."[20]

A few months later Sumner Welles, then Under-Secretary of State, declared in an address to American educators: "It should be emphasized that it is the very definite view of the Department that in this country the initiative for cultural exchange properly resides with you and that the major function of the Division is to make the good offices of the Government available to you. The concept of an 'official' culture is altogether alien to us." He continued that the Division was "essentially a clearing-house, a coordinating agency, whose purpose is to collaborate in every appropriate way without trespassing upon and much less supplanting your activities."[21] Thus, in this official view, private activity was assigned a dominant role in transnational cultural relations, with government serving to facilitate and supplement. It was hoped that the government could assist private organizations by advice on the basis of its over-all view, by helping to remove duplication of endeavor, and by coordinating activities to achieve more constructive results.

As one of various steps to secure advice and counsel from representative persons and groups outside the government, the Secretary of State in October, 1938, appointed a small Advisory Committee on Cultural Relations, already mentioned. This group was subsequently enlarged and other advisory committees were appointed on exchange fellowships and professorships, adjustment of foreign students, agricultural education, art, and music. These committees met on the average of once or twice a year; they were consulted on all important policy questions and on all major phases of the developing program. They served to keep the Department in touch with the thinking of influential leaders and groups in many fields of activity and in all parts of the country; they provided mature and seasoned counsel; and their members helped to interpret the official program to the people of the United States.

An even broader opportunity for consultation was provided by four conferences on inter-American cultural relations called by the Secretary of State in the fall of 1939. More than one thousand leaders of educational and other cultural activities came to Washington at their own expense from all sections of the United States to participate in these conferences on art, music, publications and libraries, and education. The largest of this series of conferences was that devoted to education, which brought together over 600 university and college presidents and other educational leaders from 46 states. The conference divided into six different groups to take up specific problems, such as ways of stimulating greater exchange of students, teachers, and professors; programs for academic and public education in inter-American affairs; the adjustment of foreign students; presentation in the United States of the writings of scholars and writers of the other American republics; cooperative projects in medical research and public health; curriculum materials in primary and secondary schools for Latin American studies; and teacher exchanges.

The findings and recommendations of each of the conferences were considered by continuation committees and transmitted to those attending for future study and action. These conferences rendered signal service in enlisting the interest and support of important leaders in various sections of the country.

The subsidiary role originally envisaged for the government was made abundantly clear by the meager funds allotted to the Division of Cultural Relations. As already indicated, it was given at the start approximately $28,000 for the salaries of its five officers and other staff, and nothing more.[22] One hundred dollars was made available by administrative action for the expenses of the four 1939 conferences.

A subsequent development was the transfer of government funds to individual private agencies, to finance specific tasks they undertook to do on contract. This procedure was first applied by the Office of the Coordinator of Inter-American Affairs (discussed later). For example, the Institute of International Education played a leading role in student exchange. The distribution of books in English on the United States to libraries abroad was administered by the American Library Association, as was also the supervision of three American libraries established in Mexico, Nicaragua, and Uruguay. Funds for assistance to American schools in Latin America were administered by the American Council on Education. Responsibility for translating English-language books into Spanish and Portuguese and vice versa was assigned to Science Service, Inc. When a system of grants to American colleges in the eastern Mediterranean area was initiated in 1943, the funds were handled by the Near East College Association.

Thus, through advisory committees, conferences, informal consultation, frequent addresses and articles, and finally a system of contract grants, a working partnership between government and private organizations, both representing the people of the United States, was developed and maintained. Through these means the cultural cooperation program was given in the United States a broad democratic base, which helped to make more representative its presentation of the American way of life.

Finally, what of the objectives of the two agencies set in motion in 1938, and the relation of those objectives to United States foreign policy? In the thought of many officials of the Department of State, the cultural program was viewed as a measure to advance the Good Neighbor policy in Latin America, and designed in large part to counteract the Axis drive in the other American republics. The purpose of the Interdepartmental Committee was through understanding and cooperation "to develop and strengthen inter-American political solidarity, and the economic and social well-being of the Americas."[23]

But some officers of the Division of Cultural Relations and their private advisers were chary of adopting any "ulterior" objective for a program of cultural relations. Some held the same view as that phrased in 1943 in the statement, "Any implication of a tie-in between cultural interchange and foreign policy invalidates the effect of cultural activities."[24] Cultural exchange should be pursued for its own sake—a tenet stemming from the earlier period when the transnational cultural activities of the United States were carried on primarily by private organizations and individuals. The cultural program was not to be a propaganda effort, in "the sense of penetration, imposition, and unilateralism." It should emphasize reciprocity, which was considered essential in cultural relations. The program was to be definitely educational in character.[25]

The relation of the cultural program to United States foreign policy was reviewed at some length by the General Advisory Committee in February, 1943. The discussion was stimulated by a broad proposal for a postwar program in the cultural field, presented by Ralph E. Turner. On the one hand, members of the Committee pointed out that to use cultural relations merely as a tool of political and economic policy would be to defeat the essential purposes of the program. It was contended that cultural relations would better advance the security of the American people indirectly rather than directly, that is, by directing them toward stimulating free cultural development on the international level, thus providing a favorable world climate for the growth of international peace and security and hence the security of the American people. On the other hand, it was argued that since the foreign policy of a nation encompassed all the relationships of its people with other peoples, a cultural program could not conceivably be conducted unrelated to general foreign policy. After extended debate, the Committee approved a statement that sought to reconcile the two points of view. It proposed that to the degree that United States foreign policy sought to achieve mutual international understanding, and to pursue as goals the free exchange of ideas and information, and a peaceful, secure, and cooperative world order, cultural relations could serve to implement that policy.[26] The negative side of this proposition was filled in by the General Advisory Committee in a resolution approved in June, 1944, when it declared: "No program of international cultural relations should be an instrument by means of which one people attempts to impose its ideas or conceptions upon another, or to achieve cultural ascendency, or to accomplish non-cultural objectives." Correlatively, "programs of international cultural relations must be collectively agreed upon as between peoples and must be mutually acceptable and reciprocally carried out."[27]

Thus during this initial period two divergent views emerged as to the relation of the governmental program of cultural relations to United States foreign policy. One argued that the program should be valid in its own right and not viewed as an instrument for forwarding political and economic policy. The other considered it as inevitably and closely linked to those phases of foreign policy. Both schools professed recognition of the importance of reciprocity in cultural relations. The emphasis of the program should be on education as distinguished from "propaganda." Its impact was long-term rather than immediate. Private organizations in addition to government agencies should play a leading role, and the program should represent the interests of the American people as well as of their government.

These early programs were of a pioneering and ground-breaking character. The exchange of persons had been earlier developed under private auspices, but even here experimentation was necessary in linking governmental participation with unofficial activities. In other activities, such as the provision of government support to cultural institutes or centers, as well as to American libraries and schools situated in foreign countries, and to cooperative projects of a technical or scientific character abroad, it was necessary to explore virgin territory. It was only after numerous questions of fundamental policy had been examined and analyzed, often at the cost of considerable delay, that future activity could flow smoothly and uninterruptedly through channels which had been marked out and cleared.

CULTURAL OFFICERS ABROAD

A new kind of diplomat—the cultural attaché or cultural officer—was bred by this new kind of government activity. It was early evident that the program required not only personnel in Washington but, of even greater importance, officers in the field, where contacts with foreign peoples were actually made. In August, 1941—three years after the Division of Cultural Relations was set up—the first such officers were appointed, most of them to our diplomatic posts in Latin America but a few to similar posts outside the Western hemisphere. Formerly only an occasional foreign service officer, because of personal interest or a special situation, had given sporadic attention to cultural matters.

The duties of the new type of officer were of every color and description, matched only by the variegated qualifications required by such a novel specialty. He was supposed to possess a broad and rounded knowledge of the social, educational, scientific, and artistic life of the United States, and of the leading public and private organizations in those areas of activity. Correspondingly, he was to inform himself of similar activities and trends in the country where he was stationed. He was called on to seek out and become acquainted with educational leaders, writers, journalists, musicians and painters, scientists, and other scholars. He assisted in the selection of students, teachers, and other persons to travel and study in the United States, and helped corresponding groups of his fellow citizens in their visits to his host country. He advised on the distribution of American books to libraries, universities, and other institutions. He kept a benevolent eye on cultural centers and American schools. He was in short the human channel or rather the human engineer who sought to make the two-way flow of cultural information and experience mutually helpful and useful.[28]

A later development was the appointment in 1951 of a limited number of scientific attachés abroad, in accordance with the recommendations of a survey group headed by Lloyd V. Berkner,[29] and the naming of a science adviser in the Department of State. These attachés were to advise on scientific matters, and to facilitate the flow of scientific information and the exchange of scientific personnel. With the advent of the Eisenhower administration in 1953 the program was gradually allowed to lapse, and was reestablished only after the launching of the first Soviet satellite in October, 1957. Since 1958 science officers have been authorized for the staffs of American embassies in Bonn, London, Paris, Rome, Stockholm, Tokyo, New Delhi, Buenos Aires, Rio de Janeiro, Bern, and Tel Aviv.

WORLD WAR II

The outbreak of war in Europe in 1939 brought new scrutiny to the cultural program. This scrutiny was intensified after the attack on Pearl Harbor and the entry of the United States into the struggle in December, 1941. The principles and program developed from 1938 on, when the United States was shifting from neutrality to strengthening national defense and preparation for possible conflict, came under reappraisal once the conflict had actually engulfed the United States. What could and should be their contribution to the war effort?

World War II had three effects on the government's cultural program. First, it sharpened recognition of the vital importance of Latin America, where official cultural activities had been concentrated, to the security of the United States. What could these activities contribute to a better knowledge of the United States and its war aims and to a greater willingness to cooperate on the part of the republics of the area? Militarily, Latin America was an exposed flank of the United States—a flank that required dependable allies for its defense against infiltration and possible invasion.

Latin America was a near-by source of strategic materials, all the more significant because of Nazi submarine ravages on ocean shipping. The war cut off shipments of natural rubber from Asia, and thus gave urgency to efforts under the Interdepartmental Committee to expand its production in Latin America. Cooperative surveys to locate and make available such minerals as manganese, chromium, tungsten, and tin took on added significance when war demands gave these materials increased strategic value. Cooperation with Latin America in weather forecasting was of importance to military as well as civil aviation. The training of pilots by the Civil Aeronautics Administration enabled the other republics to replace former Axis personnel with their own nationals. Thus the United States stood to gain far more than formerly from such activities.

It was evident that the war would disrupt the normal channels for cultural interchange between Latin America and Europe. Travel would be severely curtailed. Scholars and scientists in Latin America would be unable to maintain their traditional contacts with Europe. Opportunities for professional training in Europe for medicine, law, and engineering, as well as for the sciences and other phases of education, would be cut off. It would therefore be important to broaden the channels for travel and communication between North and South America. The exchange of students, teachers, and professors would need to be expanded, and the doors of universities and colleges in the United States opened wider to visitors from the other American republics. Correlatively, the people of the United States required more knowledge and understanding of the peoples of Latin America.

The world conflict strengthened pressures for cultural activities to contribute immediately and directly to foreign policy objectives, and specifically to the aims of the war effort. Recognition of the contribution of cultural relations to the Good Neighbor policy, to inter-American political solidarity, and to a favorable attitude toward the United States became more pointed. These relations were viewed as enhancing the national prestige of the United States. They could serve as an antidote to Axis propaganda.[30]

At the same time, some officers of the Division of Cultural Relations held that in war as well as in peace, the long-range objectives of the cultural program should be kept in mind. Reciprocity should continue to be emphasized. The cooperation of private agencies would continue to be essential. It was recognized that war would entail a large-scale propaganda effort on the part of the United States, and that such propaganda would be directly and primarily concerned with winning the war. But, it was argued, cultural relations should be kept separate from the agencies charged with propaganda. Such relations were concerned basically with the normal and continuing aspects of the nation's life, including attention to what would be the character and needs of the postwar situation.[31]

The General Advisory Committee on Cultural Relations at a meeting in February, 1942, less than three months after Pearl Harbor, declared that it "conceives the program of cultural relations as a long-term program of continuing activities, which should, however, be realistically adaptable to changing circumstances and needs, whether in normal times or in times of emergency." While, in its view, war conditions did not call for change in the essential character or objectives of the program, it did require certain adjustments and changes of emphasis. The Committee recommended intensification of cultural interchange "as a means of strengthening resistance to attack on intellectual and cultural freedom and of reinforcing moral unity among free peoples."[32]

The Committee also looked ahead to the need of helping the war-devastated and occupied countries in rebuilding their schools and universities, their libraries and museums, and of planning for a permanent international agency in the field of education, science, and the arts. It pointed out the need of efforts to protect and preserve art treasures, historical monuments, and other cultural resources, which were threatened with damage or destruction during the conflict.[33]

Finally, the war led to a marked expansion of the government's cultural exchange program, although this expansion was small in comparison with the gigantic enlargement of activities for information and propaganda. Although, as will later be noted, the cultural activities of the Department of State underwent considerable expansion, the principal increase took place in the programs of two newly created agencies, the Coordinator of Inter-American Affairs and the Office of War Information, to which we shall now turn.

COORDINATOR OF INTER-AMERICAN AFFAIRS (CIAA)

The cultural program sponsored by the Department of State through both the Division of Cultural Relations and the Interdepartmental Committee, originally planned as a long-term activity to develop slowly and gradually and allotted only limited funds, came to be regarded as inadequate even before the United States entered the war.

By 1930 the international situation was deteriorating rapidly. In August of that year Nelson Rockefeller was appointed to head a new agency as Coordinator of Inter-American Affairs.[34] It was familiar gossip in Washington that the White House favored creation of the new agency as likely to exhibit greater imagination and drive than the Department of State. Its basic purpose was hemisphere defense. Bulking largest in its original range of responsibility were economic and information activities, the latter through press, radio, and motion pictures. In practice, commercial and financial matters were mainly handled by other government bodies. Cultural relations were included in the Coordinator's program at the suggestion of President Roosevelt himself.[35] The agency was given an initial grant of approximately $3.5 million, an amount which grew to more than $60 million for 1943 and $30 million for 1944.[36] Of CIAA total funds, less than 10 per cent were expended for cultural activities in the narrower sense.

The Coordinator and his top-level associates, many of whom had come into government service after extensive experience in private life with cultural as well as business affairs, viewed cultural activities as one element in an over-all program to advance the objectives of United States foreign policy. They enlisted wide cooperation from private groups, while energetically expanding the role of government in stimulus, sponsorship, and operation. Imagination and vigor marked their pioneering of new activities. Their first-hand knowledge of private activities in the fields of painting, music, theater, and ballet served to complement the cooperative relations developed by the Department of State with the educational organizations of the United States.[37] Thus the modest cultural operations of the Department were supplemented and extended by the Coordinator's proposals for more active exchange of persons (particularly journalists and broadcasting personnel), for distribution of American books abroad, for a reciprocal plan of translations, for assistance to United States cultural institutes and libraries and American schools in Latin America, and for exchanges in the fields of art and music.

The activities of the two agencies clearly overlapped, although an attempt at distinction was made by labeling the Coordinator's efforts as "emergency" in character, in contrast to the longer-term endeavors of the Department of State. The course of true cooperation between the two bodies ran more smoothly than outsiders at times would believe. Largely responsible for this relative harmony was a Joint Committee on Cultural Relations, composed of one representative of each of the two agencies and Waldo G. Leland, Director of the American Council of Learned Societies, serving as an informal spokesman for private organizations. The Committee met regularly from 1941 to 1945. It helped to maintain a meeting of minds on basic policy and on the character of activities undertaken.

Recognition that the cultural relations program would be a continuing element in United States foreign policy led to the transfer from the Coordinator to the Department in July, 1943, of the bulk of the former's cultural activities. An earlier proposal in May, 1941, to this effect had not been accepted.[38] This move, however, did not signify abandonment by the Coordinator of all activities that might be considered cultural in character. Programs for preparation of qualified Latin Americans for the Coordinator's programs of health, sanitation, and food supply, including grants for training in the United States, were continued, as well as certain other activities. In addition, the Coordinator took steps to develop a new inter-American educational program. This was focused on the primary and secondary levels (leaving to the Department of State responsibility for the higher or university level) and gave special attention to such fields as vocational training, health, literacy, and rural education. The Coordinator created in 1943 a government corporation, the Inter-American Educational Foundation, to receive funds and to carry on activities for a period of three to five years or longer. In 1942 the Institute of Inter-American Affairs had similarly been established for health and food activities.[39]

A unique instrument developed by the Institute of Inter-American Affairs was the *servicio*. The Coordinator's activities in agriculture, health, and primary and secondary education were conceived as joint operations, in which the United States participated cooperatively with one of the other American republics. It was believed that working together on problems of immediate concern was the most direct road to effective results as well as to understanding and friendship. The device that made possible close and constant cooperation was the *servicio,* a cooperative service set up within the appropriate ministry of the host government, but with a semiautonomous status. It was jointly financed, jointly administered, and developed joint plans that were jointly put into operation. This scheme for "doing the job together" has been successful in a number of countries, particularly where both the host government and the United States technical mission were willing to make the requisite effort to achieve a truly cooperative relationship.[40]

Mr. Rockefeller and his colleagues put forth considerable effort to develop a knowledge of the "other Americans" on the part of the people of the United States, the reciprocal phase of his activities in Latin America. A series of "Inter-American workshops" helped primary and secondary teachers prepare plans and materials relating to Latin America. Institutes and lecture series were held in various universities. The teaching of Spanish and Portuguese was encouraged. Inter-American centers were established in a number of cities throughout the country to assist local organizations in activities directed toward better inter-American understanding.[41]

OFFICE OF WAR INFORMATION

The Office of War Information, set up in 1942 with Elmer Davis as its head, more or less backed into cultural activities. Its domestic operations were overshadowed by those abroad, where it had the world for its field with the exception of Latin America, where the Coordinator of Inter-American Affairs carried on, among other things, activities similar to those of OWI elsewhere. It was a war agency designed to carry on information and propaganda activities, and psychological warfare. OWI used chiefly the mass media—press, radio, and motion pictures. Its outposts or field offices abroad served primarily as distribution centers for the products of the mass media—a news file, publications, and photographs, and a stock of motion pictures. Its task was defined as "to facilitate the development of an informed and intelligent understanding, abroad, of the status and progress of the war effort and of the war policies, activities, and aims of the Government."[42]

OWI used cultural activities primarily as an instrument to get a hearing for and to supplement its information activities. To this end it carried on three kinds of cultural projects. First, it fostered on a small scale the travel of individuals. It encouraged foreign journalists and radio commentators as well as other shapers of public opinion to visit the United States and see at first hand its war effort and way of life. Groups of Belgian, Danish, Dutch, French, Norwegian, Swedish, Iranian, and Turkish journalists were brought to this country. At the request of the British Ministry of Information it sent a small number of representative Americans from various fields of activity to interpret to British audiences the problems and achievements of America at war. Other lecturers were sent to Australia, New Zealand, South Africa, and France. Icelandic, Norwegian, and other students were invited to the United States.

Second, it provided books and magazines to supplement its news services. It developed a large program for the circulation abroad of American books and other publications, both in English and in translation. In addition to volumes bearing directly on the war aims of the United States, it arranged for cheap editions of such books as Carl Van Doren's *Benjamin Franklin* and David E. Lilienthal's *TVA: Democracy on the March*. The people of Europe as they were liberated demonstrated a voracious appetite for the many kinds of publications from which they had been barred by totalitarian censorship. OWI digest magazines and newsletters which provided summaries of magazine articles, extracts from significant books and documents, and quotations from speeches and broadcasts, helped avid readers to catch up with scientific, literary, and artistic advances, and the trends of economic, social, and political thought in the United States.

Third, OWI set up 28 information libraries in connection with its outposts abroad. These collections contained a wide range of books on the history, life, and thought of the United States—biographies, histories, American literary classics, works in the fields of economics, politics, and sociology, source books in science and technology, textbooks in medicine, and government documents, reports, and periodicals. They were intended largely for the use of editors, scholars, and public officials. Other audiences were reached by exhibits such as "America Builds" on architecture in the United States, and "Wisconsin Dairy Farmer."

One of the most useful if less dramatic of OWI undertakings was response to requests for specialized information of the widest conceivable variety from teachers, scholars, and professional men overseas. There was equal interest among organizations and individuals in the United States to renew and develop specialized ties abroad. The American Forestry Association was eager for information on the condition of forests in Europe. The Future Farmers of America, an organization of high-school boys, wished to exchange publications with similar groups abroad. The National Braille Press offered to send limited quantities of its publications free of charge to foreign schools for the blind. With the progressive liberation of Axis-occupied countries, these requests increased in number and variety. Meeting them resulted in the restoration of many lines of communication that had been severed by the war.[43]

The story of OWI is primarily one of information and propaganda, carried out mainly through the mass media. Other cultural activities were used only sporadically, in the main during OWI's concluding period of work. Libraries were the most widely supported enterprise. In some individual situations cultural cooperation became a significant element in the OWI program.

When John Gilbert Winant was named ambassador to Great Britain in 1941 he quickly came to the conclusion that the British people were not adequately informed about the United States. At his urging the OWI developed, alongside its mass media operations, information services to book and magazine publishers, schools and universities, the Board of Education, women's groups, labor unions and cooperatives, and the educational branches of the British armed forces. British publishers brought out editions of American books. His Majesty's Stationery Office, the government publishing house, agreed to republish and promote the circulation of a number of American official documents, whose sale in Britain was in some cases ten times greater than in the United States. American lecturers, as already noted, spoke to hundreds of British audiences and also over the BBC.

But the heart of the operation was the American Library, established in December, 1942, as an arm of the American Embassy. Stocked with reference books, government documents and reports, pamphlets, and current issues of general and technical American magazines, it carried on an outgoing information and reference service to Cabinet ministers and other government officials, editors, writers, educators, and students. Each book or other publication received was scrutinized to ascertain which four or five persons would find it most useful, and these were promptly advised that it was available. As the Library's director, Richard H. Heindel, observed, it was difficult to say whether the greatest contribution of this and other American libraries abroad was "national or international, current or long-term."[44]

In Iceland cultural activities helped to open the way for an information program. The peace-minded Icelanders objected to the presence of the relatively large American forces that had been landed to guard the island against Nazi occupation. They were inclined to view Americans as "boorish characters out of Western films." The Icelandic radio station was cool to the introduction of American broadcasts on its program. Opposition began to melt, however, when an art historian, who was a member of the OWI group, agreed to lecture on art, including American painting, at the Icelandic university. American classical recordings were made available to the local radio station. American books, magazines, and feature stories were provided to editors and educators. Documentary films and newsreels were shown in towns and villages. Concerts were given by musicians in the American forces. Iceland's leading actress was starred in a drama whose cast was made up of American personnel. Newsletters on agriculture, the arts, education, medicine, and science excited the interest of the well educated Icelanders. A member of the Icelandic Parliament once justified to the head of the OWI staff the distrust of his fellow countrymen toward the American forces by the remark, "We are a tiny nation, and suspicion is our navy." When the OWI leader was ending his tour of duty, he was given a farewell dinner, at which the parliamentary deputy proposed a toast to the American Information Service, "which has sunk the Icelandic navy."[45]

EXTENSION OF DEPARTMENT OF STATE PROGRAM

The war also brought a geographical expansion of the cultural activities of the Department of State from Latin America to China in 1942 and to the Near East in 1943, both financed from the President's Emergency Fund. Through the China program study grants enabled most of the 1,700 Chinese students stranded in the United States to complete their studies, professors were interchanged, copies in microfilm of technical and scholarly journals were sent to the beleaguered universities of China, and a score or more of American technical experts in agriculture, communications, engineering, and public health were sent out at the request of the Chinese government. One of these was Dr. Theodore P. Dykstra of Beltsville, Maryland, who made what was termed "perhaps the most significant American contribution to China's wartime agriculture." He took with him seven sacks of potatoes containing some fifty champion varieties. At the railroad station in Washington, the porter first refused the potatoes admission to the Pullman car, but later relented to the extent of bedding down the sacks with the traveler in an upper berth. In the course of the sea voyage, the ship was disabled off South Africa, but the potatoes were safely brought to land, and then flown the full length of Africa and across Asia to Chungking, where testing revealed the types that would give the highest production in Chinese soil.[46]

In the Near East the chief activity took the form of financial grants to American-founded nonsectarian colleges in the area, including American University at Beirut and Robert College at Istanbul, for special projects in agriculture, engineering, and health education.[47]

Under the harsh spur of war, the government's program of cultural relations was materially expanded, with mounting emphasis on its contribution to the war effort, as one means of winning and holding favorable attitudes among foreign peoples. Even so, it was dwarfed by the larger growth, many times over, of information and propaganda activities. In the programs of the war agencies, the propaganda emphasis was clearly dominant. It was less obvious and more indirect in the cultural activities of the Department of State. The character of the cultural program was modified somewhat to meet the demands of the war situation. Such activities as the exchange of journalists and specialists and the overseas libraries were put under pressure to produce immediate as well as long-term effects. Cultural relations were largely, though not entirely, viewed as one more channel for propaganda, or at least as preparing the way for propaganda.

Most of the government's cultural activities were relatively well executed, given the conditions prevailing. Experimentation and improvisation led of course to mistakes and errors. Many projects were hastily conceived and imperfectly carried out. But the personnel employed was often of high caliber—dedicated, intelligent, and hard-working. Moreover, the cultural program despite its expansion was not so large as to drain the personnel and material resources available. The government's cultural activities during World War II were in the main welcomed rather than resented by the receiving countries. Their sudden cessation or reduction at the end of the conflict caused more unfavorable reaction than their prosecution during its course.

THREE

Impact of
the Cold War: 1945-1953

WITH THE ENDING of World War II the question was raised whether the United States government should revert to its traditional policy of nonintervention in overseas information activities and indirect or limited participation in transnational cultural affairs. Never before in peace time had government agencies systematically attempted to provide information to foreign peoples. During World War I the Creel Committee on Public Information had sought to carry to Allied peoples, to neutral nations, and to enemy countries the story of American war aims and efforts. But its activities were abruptly ended on June 30, 1919.[1] Subsequently, American diplomats abroad had to a modest degree cultivated foreign journalists and provided information to increased numbers of individuals and groups on the United States and its viewpoint. But such activities were usually unsystematic and casual. While informal encouragement was given to cultural exchanges, until 1938 these were mainly left to private hands. In 1939, as we have seen, permanent authorizing legislation had been approved by the Congress for the cultural activities of the Department of State in Latin America, including the program of the Interdepartmental Committee. But their extension to the other continents as well as the continuance of a world-wide information program required further Congressional action.

Whether the war-time information program should be continued beyond the end of the conflict had been considered from 1943 on by leaders in OWI and CIAA as well as by others both inside and outside government. The question was given a temporary answer by President Truman's Executive Order (No. 9608) of August 31, 1945, which established in the Department of State an Interim International Information Service, to which were transferred the sharply reduced overseas informational activities of the two war-time agencies. The President's statement accompanying the Order declared: "The nature of present-day foreign relations makes it essential for the United States to maintain informational activities abroad as an integral part of the conduct of our foreign affairs." The Secretary of State was requested to study the needs of the postwar situation and to recommend what activities should be continued. The future program was not to compete with private agencies nor with the information services of other nations. It was to provide "a full and fair picture of American life and of the aims and policies of the United States Government."[2] A little earlier, in December, 1944, the increasing significance of informational and cultural affairs had been recognized by the creation in the Department of State of the post of Assistant Secretary in charge of public and cultural affairs, with Archibald MacLeish as the first incumbent.

As of January 1, 1946, an Office of International Information and Cultural Affairs (OIC) was set up in the Department of State under Assistant Secretary William Benton, who had succeeded Archibald MacLeish. His experience and signal success in private life as advertising executive, vice-president of the University of Chicago, publisher of the Encyclopedia Britannica, producer of educational motion pictures, and purveyor of recorded music provided a broad and varied background for this task in government. The new Office included five operating divisions, two of which, on "exchange of persons" and on libraries and cultural institutes, took over activities earlier conducted by the Division of Cultural Relations.[3] The remaining three had to do respectively with radio, press and publications, and motion pictures. To them were bequeathed the information operations formerly carried on by OWI, CIAA, and on a small scale by the Department of State itself.

The basic policy for the future program was sketched by Mr. Benton in October, 1945, in testimony before the House Committee on Foreign Affairs. He contended that foreign relations had ceased to be merely ruler-to-ruler or even government-to-government contacts. The peoples of the world were exercising mounting influence on foreign policy. In consequence, governments had set up programs designed to speak to the peoples of other countries. The United States could not be indifferent to this new situation, and was obliged to give a full and fair picture of its way of life and its foreign policies to peoples abroad. Its program should not be a miscellany of good-will activities but must be designed "to support United States foreign policy in its long-range sense and to serve as an arm of that policy." However, since the vast majority of international information and cultural exchange activities were private in character, the role of the government should be primarily to facilitate and supplement. The fundamental aim of the program was to advance the cause of peace through fostering clearer reciprocal understanding between the people of the United States and those of other nations.[4]

Postwar Reaction Favors Cultural Activities over Propaganda

But with hopes that the world was entering a period of peace and that the Soviet Union would continue in the United Nations its wartime cooperation with the Western powers, the climate for a time was more propitious for support of cultural than of information activities. Two moves approved by the Congress in 1946 enlarged the participation of the United States government in transnational cultural relations. One was the Fulbright Act relating to the exchange of students and professors. The other made the United States a member of the newly established United Nations Educational, Scientific, and Cultural Organization (Unesco).

FULBRIGHT ACT

Senator J. William Fulbright had been a Rhodes scholar at Oxford and during his middle thirties had served as president of the University of Arkansas. He proposed in his bill an ingenious and constructive solution to a perplexing postwar problem.[5] Numerous foreign countries had purchased United States surplus property which the war had left on their territory. This property included, in addition to strictly military supplies, such items as machine tools, bulldozers, and stocks of food and clothing. These purchases had been of material benefit to war-devastated countries in rebuilding their economic life after the conflict. But such countries could repay in dollars only at the risk of upsetting their economies, a disaster that the United States as well as they considered it urgent to avoid.

Senator Fulbright therefore proposed that a part of these U.S. credits in foreign currencies be used for educational interchange, which could be paid for in those currencies rather than in dollars. It provided that payments on these credits be employed for "financing studies, research, instruction, and other educational activities" of Americans in foreign countries. Such payments could also be used to help finance similar activities on the part of non-Americans. But given the fact that only foreign currencies and no American dollars would be directly involved, non-Americans could be helped only in ways that such foreign currencies could pay for—for example, travel, tuition, and maintenance for study in American schools or institutions located outside the United States, or travel to and from the United States. These foreign currency funds could not be used for study, teaching, or research by foreigners in the United States. Thus the Act, because of its exclusive concern with foreign currency expenditure, might have seemed at first glance to benefit Americans more than non-Americans. This was offset, however, by generous supplements in the form of dollar grants from other funds of the U.S. government (the Smith-Mundt Program), from other governments, and from nongovernmental organizations and institutions, American and foreign. Thus by 1961 the beneficiaries of the Act numbered 17,800 Americans and 28,000 citizens of other countries, 24,600 of whom undertook their studies or professional activities in the United States.[6]

Agreements were early signed with 20 nations (increased by 1962 to 44 in all parts of the world outside the Communist bloc), the expenditure being limited to an aggregate of $20 million for any one country and to $1 million for any country in any one year. The Act set up a Board of Foreign Scholarships to select both qualified educational institutions and the persons to receive grants, and to supervise the program.[7] The Board has consisted of ten representatives of the academic community, broadly conceived, only two of whom were officers of the federal government. The same kind of cooperation was extended across the seas, where the binational character of the commissions or foundations administering the program in each country insured its mutuality and reciprocity and accounted in large part for its widespread, continued acceptance. This binational feature had been made a part of this program because of the success of the *servicios* and other cooperative mechanisms under the various earlier programs of the United States in Latin America.[8] The Fulbright program was unique in the cooperative responsibility assigned to private agencies and in the partnership role provided for the governments and peoples of foreign countries.

Although the Act as approved made no reference to any other purposes than purely educational ones, an earlier draft introduced by Senator Fulbright in September, 1945, stipulated that expenditures should be made under regulations "to conform to American foreign policy and promote better relations between the respective governments, and in accord with the program to be initiated under the Social and Economic Council of the United Nations."[9]

Senator Fulbright, in his testimony in support of the bill, cited two precedents—the Boxer indemnity and the Belgian-American Foundation. The former has already been mentioned.[10] The latter was reviewed in a letter of February 8, 1946, addressed by former President Herbert Hoover to Senator Fulbright, supporting the latter's legislation. Mr. Hoover recalled that in 1920 the Belgian-American Educational Foundation had been set up from part of the funds resulting from the liquidation of the Belgian Relief Commission. During the next 25 years, some 700 Belgian and American students had been exchanged. By 1939 almost one-fourth of the faculty members in Belgian universities, one prime minister, and six cabinet members were former participants in this exchange.

Mr. Hoover went on to outline the less widely known subsequent efforts he had made along similar lines, which had not been successful. When Secretary of Commerce in 1923, he had sought to divert to educational purposes the war debts, not exceeding $100 million for any country. Later, when President, he had endeavored to achieve a similar purpose with regard to the republics of Latin America. Still later, in 1938, he had proposed as a private citizen that the credits granted after World War I to eleven countries, most of them in eastern Europe, for relief and reconstruction should be readjusted. Payments would be converted into a fund in their own currencies, which would be used for expansion of higher education and scientific research, for scholarships in their own universities, and for exchange of graduate students, professors, and scientific information between those countries and the United States. He had declared at that time: "The cumulative effect over the years of building up a great body of influential men and women in those countries who would understand our country and believe in us would count greatly both in economic relations and in times of international emergency. And we shall have made a contribution to civilization which may be of no quick material value but which will later serve as a great monument to our foresight."[11]

While the Fulbright Act excited little attention and no opposition in the Congress, either in committee or on the floor,[12] it did stir interest across the country among educational, religious, and business organizations. The editor of a mass-circulation magazine testified that the idea behind the proposal "appeals instinctively and naturally to the American people as a whole." Answers to a public opinion poll that had asked what could be done to give the United Nations a better chance of preventing wars put educational cooperation at the head of the list.[13]

Widespread popular support for the idea of educational and other forms of international cultural cooperation was an important factor in the 1946 decision of the United States to become a member of the United Nations Educational, Scientific, and Cultural Organization. Since early in the war American educators had shown a growing interest in the educational reconstruction of the war-ravaged countries, and in the creation after the conflict of an international organization to advance cultural cooperation. Reflecting this interest were the Mundt resolution in the House of Representatives and the Fulbright-Taft resolution in the Senate, both favoring the establishment of an international education agency, which were approved in May, 1945. Following the drafting of the Unesco Constitution at London in November, 1945, it was the testimony of numerous private organizations at the hearings on United States adherence to the new organization that forced the expansion of the U.S. National Commission for Unesco from the originally proposed 30 members to a body of 100 members, of whom 60 were to represent private organizations.[14]

INFORMATION OR PROPAGANDA?

In contrast to the favorable climate of opinion prevailing in the immediate postwar period for educational exchanges and for person-to-person relationships across frontiers, the American people as well as the Congress displayed deep and determined opposition to any governmental information or propaganda activities in time of peace. The term propaganda, as noted earlier, had acquired in the United States during the 1920s and 1930s a derogatory meaning. Propaganda was looked upon as a dirty business, which might be necessary in war but should not be continued in peace. It was not considered in accord with the traditions of American foreign policy. Moreover, there was fear that the apparatus for propaganda abroad might be shifted to focus on the American people themselves, and become a dangerous instrument in domestic political struggles.

Despite widespread hostility to propaganda, there had, nonetheless, been growing recognition in the United States of the need to provide other peoples with more knowledge about the American people and a clearer picture of American foreign policy. Traditionally, the American people had believed in the inherent power of truth and in its ability to make its way without active efforts to support or forward it. But the totalitarian powers had demonstrated that they could successfully block the flow of ideas. They set up rigid obstacles to communication with their peoples through radio broadcasts, motion picture films, newspapers, magazines, and books, and to the movement of students, teachers, and leaders in varied fields. Moreover, their own internal and external propaganda falsified the picture of what was happening in their own countries, and misrepresented the policies and actions of the United States and other countries. Truth could not travel, while falsehood was given wings. The United States was thus faced with the need to take active and effective steps to counter Soviet calumny, and at the same time to present its case both to its allies and to the uncounted millions of people in Asia, Africa, and the Middle East who were awakening to a consciousness of the forces that were shaping their world and would shape their future.

A 1947 discussion in the Committee on Foreign Affairs of the House of Representatives, during the early period of the cold war, illustrated the contrasting views on the question whether the United States should carry on abroad a program of factual information or of propaganda. General George C. Marshall, then Secretary of State, strongly opposed propaganda, declaring that "the important thing is to have people believe implicitly what we say." He cited the analogy of the banker, whose transactions might involve millions of dollars but whose credit was ruined if he misappropriated five dollars. Marshall's position was supported by Assistant Secretary of State William Benton, who argued that the best course was to play the news straight and to make every effort to avoid selection and distortion. He mentioned the foreign student coming to the United States, who unavoidably would see the bad as well as the good aspects of American life. He, therefore, favored presenting abroad a "mirror" of American life rather than a "showcase" that would display only the favorable side. W. Averell Harriman, former ambassador to the Soviet Union, argued for balancing rather than slanting the presentation, citing the impact on a country where the news is controlled of information from abroad which is candid and critical.

Congressman John Davis Lodge, however, raised the question whether a dispassionate approach would be adequate. If hostile attitudes were to be combated, some selection of the facts would be inevitable. The program should seek vigorously to advance American foreign policy. The American point of view should be presented with dynamic enthusiasm, passionate conviction, and a burning faith in the American way of life. Was not propaganda, therefore, essential, although it should be more subtle and adroit than that of the totalitarian Communists?[15]

Meanwhile the U.S.S.R. was gradually revealing the direction of its policy in the postwar world. Starting in 1945 it began to demonstrate its intention to dominate eastern Europe. It set up a puppet regime in northern Iran, and soon put Greece and Turkey under pressure. It sought to exploit for its own aggrandizement the economic weakness of central and western Europe. In 1946 its propaganda attacked the United States and Great Britain as eager to enslave other peoples. By the fall of that year, talk of the danger of a third World War was becoming current. In self-defense the West moved toward a policy of containment, including maintenance of troops and bases along a sweeping arc bordering the U.S.S.R. frontiers.

Despite these events, many Americans for almost two years after the end of World War II held to the hope of "one world" and to the faith that world peace might be assured by the development of an effective system of collective security through the United Nations. They caught at almost any straw to maintain their belief that somehow the Soviet Union would continue its wartime cooperation into the postwar period.

For this reason, Assistant Secretary of State William Benton had to wage an arduous and continuing battle from 1945 to 1947 to win Congressional and public support for authorizing legislation and appropriations to keep alive a world-wide informational and cultural program. His first appropriation request for information activities (for fiscal year 1947, starting July 1, 1946) brought from the Congress approximately $20 million,[16] with an additional $5,375,000 for the work of the Interdepartmental Committee. For the 1948 fiscal year his request of $31 million for information operations was slashed by the House of Representatives to zero; but as the result of Senate action he was finally voted $12.4 million with $3.9 million additional for the Interdepartmental Committee. This was the low point.[17]

SMITH-MUNDT ACT

The House Appropriations Committee stressed, as one reason for denial of funds, the lack of authorizing legislation. Mr. Benton had inherited drafts of bills designed primarily to expand beyond Latin America the work of the Interdepartmental Committee and the cultural relations program. One such bill (H.R. 4982), sponsored by Congressman Sol Bloom, was rewritten after hearings before the Committee on Foreign Affairs and was approved by the House in July, 1946, but died in the Senate. After further revision, including addition of authorization for an information program abroad, the bill (as H.R. 3342) was introduced by Congressman (now Senator)

Karl E. Mundt and cosponsored by Senator H. Alexander Smith. It met with no opposition during committee hearings, and attracted strong support from such witnesses as General George C. Marshall, then Secretary of State; Secretary of Commerce Averell Harriman; General Dwight D. Eisenhower, then Chief of Staff; and General Walter Bedell Smith, ambassador to Moscow. It was also supported by the American Legion, the American Veterans of World War II, and the Veterans of Foreign Wars. On the floor of the House, however, it encountered strong attacks. Karl E. Mundt (Republican), who led the fight for the bill, remarked of the debate, "Never since I have been in Congress have I heard such a disorganized collection of misinformation circulated about any one piece of legislation as about this legislation."[18] Only after a debate extending over five days, in which an unusually large number of Congressmen took part, was it approved in June, 1947, by a vote of 272 to 97.

Opponents of the measure stressed the need for economy with the national debt at a peak figure, distrust of the personnel carrying on information and cultural activities, and finally stubborn disbelief in the value of the program itself. It was charged that the exchange of students and teachers would let down immigration bars and open American schools "to Communists and agitators." The proponents of the bill made frequent reference to the need of counteracting the bitter Soviet propaganda attacks on the United States, and the importance of making clear that the $12 billion contributed by the United States for feeding and reconstruction of the war-devastated countries did not represent economic imperialism as charged by the U.S.S.R.

After hearings in the Senate, the bill was reported out of committee with an amendment proposing that a joint Senate-House committee investigate the information and educational exchange program by means of a trip to Europe. Senate approval was then delayed until this committee could make its report. Almost half of the members of the Congress made trips abroad in 1946 and 1947, with opportunity for a close-up view of the cold war. They were astounded at the deliberate misrepresentation and the widespread misunderstanding of the United States. This factor was probably decisive for approval of the legislation. The bill was finally passed by the Senate in January, 1948, even before the Senate-House group had presented its formal report on its visit to 22 European countries. The report stressed the dangerous threat of the vitriolic Communist propaganda against the United States, and strongly recommended expansion of the U.S. information and cultural program.[19]

Few laws have been longer considered or more carefully examined by the Congress than the Smith-Mundt Act. It was in process of approval for two years. It was twice rewritten in committee, twice debated and approved on the House floor, and twice favorably reported by the Senate Foreign Relations Committee. The need for it was assessed by a joint Congressional committee on a two-month trip to Europe. Some fifty members of the Congress proposed more than one hundred amendments before its final passage.[20] Senator Karl Mundt has pointed out that the approval of the Smith-Mundt Act "required more days of debate and more pages of the Congressional Record to convince the majority of our colleagues . . . than the same session of Congress required to pass the Taft-Hartley Act, one of the most controversial pieces of legislation in recent years."[21]

The Smith-Mundt Act, formally termed the United States Information and Educational Exchange Act of 1948,[22] declared that its objectives were "to enable the Government of the United States to promote a better understanding of the United States in other countries, and to increase mutual understanding between the people of the United States and the people of other countries." It thus envisaged both unilateral and bilateral activities. These objectives were to be achieved through an information service to make available to foreign peoples knowledge about the United States, its people, and its foreign policies; and "an educational exchange service to cooperate with other nations" through the interchange of persons, knowledge, and skills, of developments in the field of education, science, and the arts, and through the provision of technical and other services (Section 2). Educational exchange was a term somewhat narrower but apparently more acceptable at the time than cultural relations.* Information about the participation of the United States in the United Nations was to be emphasized.

* The word "exchange" is properly speaking a misnomer. But the term has been broadened by usage beyond its former sense of the mutual giving and receiving of equivalents, to signify various organized activities for the two-way travel of students, professors, and other specialized personnel, the two-way flow of books and other materials, and cooperative projects covering both personnel and materials.

The Smith-Mundt Act crystallized in legislation certain fundamental policies for educational exchanges, which had guided cultural activities in preceding years: the principle of reciprocity, and full use of private agencies and advisers in cooperation with the resources of the federal government. Educational exchanges were to be on a reciprocal basis. Specifically emphasized was the responsibility, not of the United States, but of the other country, for reciprocity. Should any country fail to cooperate with the United States on such a basis, the Act authorized the Secretary of State to end or limit the program to the degree considered advisable (Section 201). Private agencies were to be used for these exchanges wherever possible. The Secretary was authorized "to make grants of money, services, or materials to State and local governmental institutions in the United States, to governmental institutions in other countries, and to individuals and public or private nonprofit organizations both in the United States and in other countries" (Section 801 [1]). No reference was made to reciprocity for information activities. But the latter were to be carried out to the maximum extent practicable by private agencies (Section 1005). Government activities in information were to be reduced whenever corresponding private activities were found to be adequate (Section 502).

The Act set up two advisory commissions, one on information and one on educational exchange, to present recommendations to the Secretary of State on policy and program. Each was to consist of five members, appointed by the President, by and with the advice and consent of the Senate. They were to present reports to the Secretary of State and to the Congress. The former was also to make semiannual reports to the latter.

Senator H. Alexander Smith, cosponsor of the Smith-Mundt Act, expressed the views of many members of Congress when in January, 1948, he spoke of the "campaign of vilification and misrepresentation" and the "incessant falsification" of the motives of the United States on the part of Soviet propaganda.[23] But the language of the Act itself reflected the thinking of preceding years, when the emphasis was on presenting "a full and fair picture" of the United States. It seemed to assume the existence of a peaceful world. Its thesis was that "if other people understood us, they would like us, and if they liked us, they would do what we wanted them to do."[24]

It called for a program whose effects would largely be long-range. It projected a defensive program to meet the Soviet propaganda offensive.

While Senator Smith declared that the Congress desired "a United States information and educational exchange program which can fully implement United States foreign policy," and demanded information activities to "tell the truth about Red fascism operating under the guise of communism and all other aggressive movements that endanger the peace of the world," the Act envisaged information only about the United States.[25] During immediate postwar years, the Voice of America abstained from criticism of or charges against the Soviet regime. Not until 1947 did it broadcast to Russia itself.

But, despite the language of the Act, events were shifting the emphasis from the 1946 reliance on the more deliberate, more indirect, and reciprocal use of educational, scientific, and artistic activities to media that would have a more immediate and aggressive effect. By 1949 it was clear that the Soviet bloc was closing its borders to educational exchange with the West.[26] By 1947 Greek-Turkish aid was initiated. The Truman Doctrine was announced. The Marshall Plan was launched. In the fall of 1947 came the establishment of the Cominform, and in 1948 the Communist take-over in Czechoslovakia and the Soviet blockade of West Berlin. The impact of these events was seen in the change of Congressional attitudes toward the use of broadcasting. In the 1946 Congressional debates, the Voice of America was subjected to more severe attack than any other activity; in 1947 it proved to be "the most popular, the most wanted, the most understood, and the least vulnerable."[27]

PROPOSED SEPARATION OF INFORMATION FROM OTHER CULTURAL ACTIVITIES

The growing demand for an active information program, with a strong propaganda emphasis to counter Soviet attacks, led to an attempt to lay down a line of separation between information and cultural activities, and thus keep the latter from being used as an overt propaganda vehicle. This movement got under way during the latter half of 1947, when the Smith-Mundt Act had passed the House but was still under consideration in the Senate.[28] It was led by Ben M.

Cherrington, who had served as the first chief of the Division of Cultural Relations in 1938–40,[29] and George F. Zook of the American Council on Education, with the assistance, among other organizations, of the Association of American Colleges and the National Education Association. In communications addressed to members of the Sentate Foreign Relations Committee, and particularly to Senator H. Alexander Smith, this group condemned the "mixing" of information and cultural activities, which they viewed as "distinct in purpose and emphasis," and recommended complete organizational and administrative divorcement of the two programs in the Department of State. They also urged that in foreign countries the offices carrying on educational activities should be physically separated from the embassy itself and from the information offices.

While this group of educators fully recognized the necessity and importance of the information program in a time of acute international tension, they drew, as Senator Smith came to do, a definite line between information and cultural activities. In their view information was closely involved in "politics," whereas cultural activities should be "nonpolitical." The term "political" was seemingly used in two senses. First, international information activities were viewed as tied up with "power politics." They were employed as an instrument "to implement the diplomatic policies of the Department of State." As channeled through radio, press, and motion pictures, they were largely unilateral in character, and might smack of imposition. Second, on the domestic side, it was argued that American tradition favored divorcing educational, scientific, and artistic activities from the federal government, and their development rather under the auspices of private agencies and of state and local governments. Thus the role of the federal government, and particularly of the Department of State, should be a strictly secondary one, limited to stimulus, facilitation, and coordination.

Further, it was contended that information, "no matter how accurate and fair it may be, . . . always will be interpreted by citizens of other countries as the propaganda of the U.S. government." Cultural activities should be kept clear of propaganda, otherwise they might be viewed as cultural imperialism designed to impose the culture of the United States on other peoples.

An additional distinction advanced was that information was

mainly concerned with immediate, day-to-day matters, whereas cultural activities had to do with more permanent and enduring elements in the American way of life.

Positively, it was argued that international cultural cooperation should "involve reciprocity and mutuality of interests" and that it succeeds only as it enlists "the cooperative spirit of mankind." It involves partnership and sharing. The essentially international (rather than nationalistic) attitude of these educators emerged in the view, expressed by Dr. Cherrington, that not only cultural but also information activities would be more in keeping with American ideas and traditions if carried on under an international agreement, prescribing standards and principles which would be accepted by all nations engaging in such activities. He declared: "Were this possible the distinction between information and educational exchange might become largely academic." Unesco, for example, combined in its program with little difficulty or question both education and mass communication, because the two were equally part of a cooperative international enterprise. Thus the basic distinction in the minds of this group seems to have been whether an activity sought to serve a unilateral nationalism or a multilateral partnership.

One summary of the position of the educators was given by Senator H. Alexander Smith when he said in a floor debate, "Educational exchange service . . . to be truly effective, must be objective, nonpolitical, and above all have no possible propaganda implications." Separation would permit the educational program, in the restrained language of Senator Smith, "to remain undisturbed" during a time when the information service might be in for some strenuous and grimy propaganda jobs.

It may be noted that the information program had in the past regarded cultural activities as a useful if somewhat minor adjunct. The divorce was sought rather for the benefit of the objectives of the cultural program. Any discernible mixing of propaganda intent with the objectives of cultural cooperation, it was argued, would thwart the purpose of the government's cultural activities.[30]

The proponents of separation did not demand a different agency for cultural relations outside the Department of State. But within the Department they wished to extend the division up to the top layer of active direction, having two Assistant Secretaries, one specially qualified for education and the other for information. However, the Congressional supporters of the legislation contented themselves with envisaging separate offices, or "services" as they were referred to in the Act, for educational exchange and information, both under the Assistant Secretary; and by prescribing the creation of two advisory commissions. It was also hoped that activities abroad, while under the direction of the United States ambassador, would "fall into two distinct and separate categories—educational and informational." Some balance should be maintained as to the size of the two activities but the Congress did not wish to legislate on administrative patterns either in the Department of State or in the field.[31]

How effectively did the attempt at separation work out? The division between the areas of activity was more distinct in Washington than in the field. In the latter area cultural officers who originally had been on the staff of the embassies proper were grouped with information officers in what was called the United States Information Service. Its title illustrates the fact that with the cold war dominating the international scene, educational exchange was massively overshadowed by the information program and reduced, administratively, to a "media service" thereof. Information received the major share of the budget and the bulk of attention. Moreover, both in Washington and in the field, men trained in journalism, public relations, and advertising were as a rule in the top positions, and thus in direction and control of men trained in education and similar fields who were carrying on cultural activities.

Ex-Enemy Countries

In the meantime, United States cultural and information activities were involved in a special situation in the countries defeated in World War II. Germany, Austria, and Japan were treated as ex-enemy countries, but Italy and Korea were viewed rather as "liberated areas." The two latter countries, while formally under military occupation, were prompted to set up their own governments and to develop their own international relations. Our attention here will center on Germany and Japan, as most fully exemplifying the problems to be discussed.

There were important differences in the two occupations: Germany under four-power control, Japan actually under dominant United States rule, despite formal Allied supervision; the German government completely shattered, the Japanese remaining intact; the German occupation lasting ten years (1945–55),[32] the Japanese seven years (1945–52). But certain common elements characterized both situations. The experience of the United States with cultural and information activities in these two ex-enemy countries was particularly significant for several reasons.

In the first place, the United States enjoyed far more authority in these countries than in others where information and cultural programs operated. The relation was that of victor to vanquished. Domination and coercion were inherent in the situation. But these approaches were early recognized as inadequate. If changes were to be achieved in education and other cultural fields, the consent of the subjugated peoples was essential. Their cooperation had to be attained.

Second, although the United States government could in theory act alone, without the collaboration of private agencies either in the United States or in the occupied countries, in practice private agencies early assumed an influential role. In the United States, the Commission for International Educational Reconstruction (CIER) marshaled from 1946 to 1949 an impressive degree of private effort, which included, along with aid to the nations devastated by the Axis powers, attention to educational problems in the occupied countries. In 1946 two missions composed primarily of distinguished private educators visited Germany and Japan to make recommendations to the United States government. Subsequently the Commission on the Occupied Areas (COA) served from 1948 to 1951 to stimulate and coordinate voluntary activities, to advise the government on education and other cultural affairs, and on occasion and at governmental request to operate certain programs.[33] In a somewhat more limited role, private agencies in Germany and Japan carried out important activities.

Third, the objectives of United States information and cultural activities in Germany and Japan were far more ambitious than those normally sought through cultural relations with other countries. With the initial stage marked by steps to eliminate militaristic and

totalitarian influences in schools and universities, as well as in book
and magazine publishing, radio, press, and films, the underlying goal
was to lay the foundations for democracy and to this end to reeducate
the conquered peoples. But it did not take long to recognize the impossibility of achieving these objectives by short-term measures. The
anomaly of a democracy attempting to impose democracy and reeducation by military occupying forces soon became evident. In addition,
the rapid resurgence of the German and Japanese peoples made clear
that such goals were outdated in the actual situation. They were then
superseded by more modest approaches through advice and persuasion, such as working through national educators and the use of
cultural interchange to bring the occupied peoples from their war-
time isolation into touch again with the thought currents of the
rest of the world. The objective of "reeducation" was replaced by
that of mutual understanding and cooperation.[34]

Fourth, the size of the information and cultural program, particularly in Germany, was unprecedented. At one time it topped the
proportions of such activities in all other countries combined. In Japan the mass of direct Occupation projects never became so prepon-
derant because many activities were carried out by the Japanese government itself.

Valid conclusions are not readily harvested from a review of the
cultural activities sponsored by the Occupation authorities. It is
highly difficult to identify the slowly maturing fruit of the efforts
put forth. The United States was inexperienced in the arts and sciences of military occupation. Mistakes were made and projects were
often fruitless. Various initiatives sponsored by the two Occupations
were subsequently modified or abandoned. The most significant contribution of the Occupations was the opportunity and at times the
encouragement they gave to prodemocratic forces in Germany and
Japan to assert themselves. If not too much was achieved in teaching
democracy, something was done in democratizing teaching.[35] Valuable also, especially for Germany, were the programs enabling substantial numbers of educational and other leaders to renew their contacts with the outside world.[36]

Official cultural exchanges between Germany and the United
States began in any volume only in 1948, after abandonment of the

"nonfraternization" policy which with other measures had put Germany in virtual quarantine from the rest of the world. The exchanges were originally viewed by the Occupation "as an instrument for smuggling in democratic bacteria" in the belief that "exposure to life in the United States was the best way of producing carriers and therewith contagion." [37] The number of Germans visiting the United States totaled 11,000, starting with 232 in 1948, increasing to 932 for 1949, to more than 2,400 annually for 1950 and 1951, and then declining to 2,200 for 1952, to almost 1,900 for 1953, and to 1,000 for 1954. Much smaller numbers of Americans were sent to Germany, the number falling short of 200 annually up through 1952, and then exceeding 300 each for 1953 and 1954.[38]

The most prominent programs were those bringing German leaders and experts, German students, and German teen-agers to the United States. In the selection process, German groups played a considerable role. The leaders were mature persons who had gained positions of responsibility in political life. A review indicated that at one time or another they included 25 per cent of the lower house and 17 per cent of the upper house of the German parliament; the labor movement, education, community affairs, public health and welfare, and other fields were represented. In some years more than a thousand visited the United States for periods ranging from 30 to 120 days. Similarly the number of students reached a peak of a thousand in certain years, most of them remaining for at least nine months. Several hundred German youths between the ages of 16 and 19 spent a year in the United States, each living with an American family and attending high school. The Americans sent to Germany were mostly specialists, who served in Germany as advisers and lecturers in such fields as education, community affairs, and public health and welfare.[39]

Information on the rest of the world and especially the United States was brought to the German people, cut off as they had been under the Hitler regime, through the press, radio, newsreels, and documentary films. Several hundred American books were translated and published, along with numerous pamphlets. The activity that probably attracted more overt support from the Germans than any other was the establishment of "America Houses," which were libraries and information centers providing open-shelf reading rooms, English classes, art exhibitions, film showings, concerts, and lectures. At the peak there were twenty-six of these centers.[40]

In Japan the educational policies of the Occupation for reeducation and reform were directed toward elimination of the militaristic and ultranationalistic emphases fostered before and during the war, and toward remaking Japanese society more or less in the pattern of democracy in the United States. Education was viewed as an instrument to build democracy, by developing independent thought, respect for the individual and for the rights of others, and international friendship with tolerance for people of all races and religions. Among measures strongly advocated were provision of equal educational opportunity for all, decentralization of educational control with establishment of local school boards, and the strengthening of academic freedom. These trends received legal support in the new Japanese Constitution of 1946 and the Fundamental Law of Education promulgated in 1947. Important changes were made in the curriculum. Educational opportunities were expanded, especially on the secondary level. The reforms were carried out through the Japanese government, and the Japanese people, who showed considerable zeal for change, provided a notable degree of cooperation.[41] Unfortunately, the destruction of the old mystical and nationalistic ideological structure left a spiritual vacuum, which the modern democratic creed was too vague and too unfamiliar to fill. One result was the appearance of a "lost" generation, whose members often seemed irresponsible and amoral. At the same time the craving for some form of dogmatic certainty helped Communist doctrines to win considerable ground among teachers and students. The changes advocated by the Occupation might have had greater prospect for permanence if, instead of being labeled as "new," they had been linked to traditions that antedated the war-time emphasis on militant nationalism. American influence on Japanese education had been strong in the 1870s and again after the first World War and in the 1930s.[42]

During the early years of the occupation the Japanese were barred from travel abroad by regulations and currency restrictions, except in special cases. But the value of such travel in renewing ties with the outside world and developing better understanding of the United States was somewhat tardily recognized in 1949. Between that year and 1952, 1,130 Japanese, mainly selected by Japanese agencies, received scholarships for study in the United States from GARIOA funds (Government and Relief in Occupied Areas). Private support for education abroad became available for almost an equal number. By 1952–53 some 900 Japanese were studying in the United States without any U.S. government support. Approximately 1,500 "leaders," including business executives, government officials, political figures, technicians, and educators were also sent to the United States. In the opposite direction a small number of teachers, consultants, and scholars were brought from the United States to Japan.[43] But the Japanese flow never reached the proportions of the German exchanges.

Use of information media by the Occupation was more indirect in Japan than in Germany. It did not itself employ radio broadcasting. American documentary films were widely shown by Japanese prefectural centers. The Occupation sponsored no newspapers or magazines. But its influence was pervasive through authoritative "suggestions." It pursued contradictory policies at times, seeking to foster the freedom of the Japanese press while imposing on occasion a heavy-handed censorship. Corresponding to the America Houses in Germany were information centers, belatedly introduced by SCAP, which provided books, magazines, recordings, and other cultural materials. Twenty-three were in operation by the end of the Occupation.[44] In addition a score of textbook and curriculum centers containing American material were established. American magazine and newspaper articles and more than a thousand books were translated, some American plays produced, and some performances of American musical compositions presented.[45]

Conceivably, the United States could have carried out in the ex-enemy countries a military, purely governmental, unilateral effort at cultural imposition and educational reform. But experience brought a progressive replacement of military by civilian administration, the enlistment of private American agencies to cooperate with government activities, and a growing recognition that people could be changed only with their consent, that democratic attitudes could be inculcated only by democratic methods: advice and persuasion, encouragement of indigenous effort rather than reform by fiat, collaboration rather than imposition. This change of attitude was evidenced in the initiation of the cooperative programs under the Fulbright Act in Austria in 1950, Japan in 1951, and Germany in 1952.

The weakness of the two Occupations in Germany and Japan, in relation to educational reform and cultural exchange, was their essentially authoritarian character. Purges, censorship, rough-shod rejection of national traditions—unavoidable at least in the early stages —inevitably stirred resentment and resistance. It is too much to expect that conquerors should exhibit humility and a willingness themselves to learn. But at least a more profound and consistent attempt to understand the history and basic values of the German and Japanese peoples might have suggested how desired changes could be rooted in the national way of life. Occupation officials too often rejected the knowledge they most needed. When on all too infrequent occasions thoughtful Americans sat down with their counterparts in the ex-enemy countries, they found useful ways of working together.

The relations of the United States with the Soviet Union in Germany warrant special mention. It was in Germany that the United States came into most direct contact with the suspicion and hostility of the U.S.S.R. The cold war had a marked influence on the objectives of the United States in Germany, emphasizing the need for counteracting Soviet propaganda and for providing the Germans with a better knowledge of the workings of democracy in the United States.

Korean Aggression and the Campaign of Truth, 1950

The authority to set up a world-wide program of international information and educational exchange conferred upon the Secretary of State by approval of the Smith-Mundt Act in January, 1948, came at a strategic moment. The international situation continued to deteriorate. Communist propaganda attacks on the United States grew ever more bitter. Although NATO was set up in 1949 and the Berlin blockade lifted, the Chinese Communists in a series of victories had put the forces of Chiang Kai-shek to rout and south and southeast Asia seemed threatened by a sweeping Communist advance. The cold war had clearly become global. This worsening situation culminated in the aggression against the Republic of Korea in June, 1950.

Senator William Benton in that year had said of Communist propaganda, "There has never been anything like it, anything so skillful and so effective in its mass impact." He listed five themes as central in the attacks on the United States.

First. The United States is headed for a cataclysmic economic crash.

Second. The rulers of the United States are Fascists, warmongers, and monopolists.

Third. Although the rich in the United States are getting richer, everybody else is getting poorer and there is starvation, unrest, and growing sympathy for the Soviet Union among the masses.

Fourth. America's vaunted freedom is a fraud, and our doctrine of equality is belied by racial and religious discrimination.

Fifth. Our character is bad—we are culturally barbarous, money-mad, lawless, crime-ridden, and effete.[46]

Administrative steps had been promptly taken to comply with the prescriptions of the Smith-Mundt Act. In the Department of State the Office of Educational Exchange and the Office of International Information were established under the Assistant Secretary for Public Affairs. The two corresponding Advisory Commissions were appointed.[47] But it was not until 1950 that the budget and with it the program were substantially expanded; and this was achieved only after the President of the United States had so recommended, and his recommendation had been underlined by the Korean aggression and the leadership of the United States in the resistance of the United Nations forces. These events brought with them a modification and sharpening of the concept and objectives of the educational exchange as well as of the information program.

Shortly after the first Soviet atomic explosion the National Security Council decided, in January, 1950, on the basis of a wide and thoroughgoing review, that the international situation confronting the United States was perilous, and outlined a program of strengthened defenses to meet the dangers threatening American security. The program called for enlarged and harder-hitting propaganda activity. In April President Truman underlined this proposal in a speech to the American Society of Newspaper Editors, urging a

world-wide "Campaign of Truth." [48] This title proved to be not entirely realistic. In the atmosphere of crisis, truth suffered more attri-
tion than formerly from partisan fact and slanted information. Two
months later came the aggression in Korea, accompanied by insistent
stress in Soviet propaganda on charges that the attack had been
launched by the Republic of Korea, not on it, and that the action
of the United Nations forces was offense, not defense—the "big lie"
tactic so often used by Hitler.

Plans for the "Campaign of Truth" had been laid before the beginning of the Korean aggression. They were formulated under the
direction of Edward W. Barrett, who had succeeded Ambassador
George V. Allen as Assistant Secretary of State in 1950. Support for
a large-scale expansion of international information and education to
counter aggressive Communist propaganda had come from Senator William Benton, former Assistant Secretary of State, 1945–47,
who together with twelve other Senators sponsored in March, 1950,
a bi-partisan resolution calling for a "world-wide Marshall plan in the
field of ideas." This proposal urged intensified use of radio and films,
a significant increase in the number of foreign students brought to
the United States, support through the United Nations and through
United States diplomacy for world-wide freedom of information,
and acceleration of the work of Unesco. It advocated setting up in
the United States a private agency to stimulate and guide the efforts of multitudes of individual citizens in furtherance of the international information and education programs. Finally, it demanded
that "the international propagation of the democratic creed be made
an instrument of supreme national policy. . . ." [49]

With the added stimulus of the Communist invasion of Korea in
June, 1950, the Congress appropriated in that summer greatly increased funds. In addition to the regular appropriation of $32.7 mil-
lion already approved for the 1951 fiscal year, a supplemental request
yielded an additional appropriation of $79 million plus $19.6 million
in counterpart funds. The largest increases were for mass media—
radio, press, and motion pictures. Smaller gains were made by exchange of persons, overseas libraries, and distribution and translation of books. The dollar support for the program in the 1951 fiscal
year was two and a half times that of 1950, and four times that of
1949, the first full year of operations under the Smith-Mundt Act. [50]

SHIFT IN OBJECTIVES

The Smith-Mundt Act and the activities of the Department of State thereby authorized had been grounded on the assumption that the export of accurate information about the United States would help to create an atmosphere of international understanding, which would make easier the attainment of the goals of United States foreign policy. But it had gradually become clear that Soviet hostility was the fruit not of ignorance but of deliberate intent. Moreover, the Communist attack in Korea brought into the picture another factor that earlier had not been sharply recognized—the need to counter the "intensive campaign for the conversion of whole peoples to the Communist point of view," as exemplified by North Korea prior to the 1950 aggression.[51]

In consequence the "Campaign of Truth" was to be a psychological offensive against Soviet propaganda activities and in favor of a more positive attitude on the part of other peoples toward the United States. Its stated objectives were to strengthen cohesion among the countries of the free world, to present the United States as a worthy partner with whom to cooperate, to deter Communist aggression, and to help roll back Soviet influence.[52]

Acceptance of the new strategy involved a more precise formulation of tactics. Previously the plan of operations had been primarily to assemble and send out for world distribution news and information about the United States. But not infrequently the story presented had overwhelmed and disconcerted foreign peoples, and by its portrayal of American prosperity and of the superior comfort and well-being of the American standard of living had stirred resentment. At times an approach that had stimulated a favorable response in one group or country had called forth an opposing one elsewhere. The new offensive led to three changes: the classification of different countries on the basis of their strategic importance to the United States campaign; the selection in each country of target groups; and the choice of the most effective materials and media for reaching those groups.[53] High officials now spoke openly of both information and educational exchange as propaganda, but insisted that both were truthful. International information and educational exchange were included among the "United States programs for national defense," outlined by the National Security Council and approved by the President on October 18, 1951. As such they were to be integrated with the military and economic programs of national defense.[54]

The emphasis in the campaign on a unilateral approach and the shift from stress on mutual understanding to efforts to persuade other peoples to support U.S. objectives were brought to bear on educational exchanges and other cultural activities, as well as on the information program. Increasingly ignored were the distinctions laid down in the Smith-Mundt Act between the two fields of activities, and Congressional recommendations for maintaining a balanced program. As earlier indicated, the thinking of men with a journalistic or advertising background dominated budgetary and administrative planning for cultural as well as for information activities. Although the former activities were more resistant than the latter to the pressures for a campaign of national propaganda, they too underwent some modification in objectives, involving compromises with earlier principles.[55]

The Advisory Commission on Educational Exchange had recognized in 1949 that a basic problem facing the program of cultural activities was the lack of agreement on its objectives. It listed four different interpretations.

According to one view the purpose of this program is to transplant American methods and techniques to other countries, to "Americanize" them, in fact, as one representative stated it. A second view is that its purpose is to acquaint other nations with the accomplishments of the United States in the fields of scholarship and the fine arts in order to impress them with our cultural achievements. A third view is formulated in altruistic terms: this program is to help other countries meet their problems of education and should be guided, therefore, by local needs. A fourth view sees the educational exchange program as a special form of the information program of the State Department. It would weigh each undertaking only in terms of its immediate impact, as well as our foreign policy objectives in a particular country at the time.[56]

In response to these varying interpretations the Commission declared that the program was not "an effort to 'Americanize' other nations." Such a policy, the Commission noted, "could be successful only until it were found out." The objective of the program was not "to make friends for the United States." While international friendship was obviously desirable, the Commission remarked that there was "no short cut to genuine friendship. Like happiness, it is a by-product of other things." In this case it should be a by-product of mutual knowledge and cooperative association. The program was not one of "beneficent educational paternalism" in the sense of seeking to take over the educational responsibilities of other countries. Nor was it a phase of the information program. It was not unilateral, but fundamentally reciprocal. It was mutually beneficial. It did not carry on propaganda for specific objectives. It rather forwarded the foreign policy of the United States "by bringing about growing understanding of American life, confidence in this country's broad objectives, and a desire to be associated with her in working toward these ends."[57] The Commission later proposed the distinction that "the information program deals primarily with immediate issues, while the educational exchange program is concerned with broader understanding of the character of American civilization, its . . . purposes, and attitudes toward other peoples."[58]

In connection with this analysis the Commission set forth, within the broad purpose outlined in the Smith-Mundt Act for increasing mutual understanding between the people of the United States and those of other countries, three more specific objectives. First, to develop awareness in other nations of the technical and economic resources of the United States as well as of the social organizations, the cultural activities, and the moral strength of the American people. Second, to provide "an understanding of the character and motives of the United States and confidence in her purposes." Third, to reveal the mutual benefits of cultural exchanges to all who take part in them.[59]

While the above objectives of educational exchange were not devoid of political content, they were brought more closely into line with the unilateral goals of the "Campaign of Truth"—after the launching of that crusade—by a restatement on the part of the Commission which defined the goals of educational exchange as keeping alive the spirit of cooperation among the free nations, strengthening resistance to Communism in countries under threat of infiltration or aggression, and weakening the power of Communism in areas under the domination of the U.S.S.R.[60]

Leading officials in charge of the educational exchange program stressed even more strongly its political objectives. For example, William C. Johnstone, Director of the Office of Educational Exchange in the Department of State from 1948 to 1952, declared: "It is basically a political job, for this program is an effective arm or instrument of American foreign policy. In its simplest form, the job of this program is to implant a set of ideas or facts in the mind of a person. When this is done effectively, it results in action favorable to the achievement of American foreign policy. It can help unite the free nations on the road to peace."[61]

EFFORTS TO REDIRECT OVERSEAS LIBRARIES AND EXCHANGE OF
PERSONS

The more directly political objectives laid down for cultural activities led to efforts to redirect specific programs, such as the overseas libraries and the exchange of persons. In November, 1950, the libraries were renamed "information centers," as indicating a "more positive role" in the distribution of books, the showing of films and exhibits, and the holding of lectures and discussion groups.[62] The translation of "politically effective" books increased fivefold, to an annual total of 2 million copies.

The library service of these information centers provides one illustration of the compromises resulting from the pressures generated by the "Campaign of Truth." On the one hand, it was considered essential to preserve the unbiased character of the book collections, which had won the confidence of their foreign readers. On the other, it was argued that their service should be focused more sharply on leadership groups in other countries and on the fields of knowledge—such as history, economics, and political science—within which the objectives of U.S. foreign policy could most effectively be furthered.

The problem of adjustment thus had two facets: the policy of book selection and the audience sought. The policy of including in the collections volumes critical of as well as favorable to the United States—in fact, the whole gamut of domestic opinion, save that of

Communist or Fascist views—was maintained. But the centers had felt the impact of pressures on the domestic scene bearing on the controversial character of certain authors. The Department of State in general withstood pressures on general policies such as the stocking of "liberal" magazines, but at times gave ground on individual titles or the writings of specific authors.

As to audience, it was obvious that the collections could in no way rival radio or press in reaching the mass of the general public. A process of natural selection limited their readers to the educated class, whose members had the interest and capacity to profit from serious works written in a foreign language. But scrutiny of the strategic usefulness of the library collections stimulated by the "Campaign of Truth" led to a definition of their most effective audience as made up of "opinion-moulders" and "decision-makers," comprising educators, authors, and journalists in the first group, and political, industrial, and labor leaders in the second.

Thus the attempt to accommodate both political and cultural objectives led to a concept of the libraries as neither a passive channel for the flow of indiscriminate information, nor an instrument for dissemination of specifically tempered or particularly colored propaganda. They were rather viewed as an honest but carefully defined means of bringing knowledge to selected groups on selected subjects.[63]

It should also be added that they functioned to serve certain selected objectives. Their purpose, as defined by the legislation in 1952, was to "promote the national security of the United States." In addition to furthering "a balanced understanding of the United States," and making available "American contributions to the humanities and to the social and physical sciences," they were to "combat anti-American propaganda; . . . interpret American foreign policy, with particular reference to Soviet aggression; and reveal the fallacy of the Communist doctrine."[64]

The program for exchange of persons also underwent modification in the "Campaign of Truth" "to serve immediate needs more effectively." Among foreign leaders brought to the United States, the proportion estimated as able to influence quickly their fellow citizens on return home was increased by 30 per cent. The purpose, as Secretary of State Dean Acheson put it, was "to work with people who will yield some results right away. You want to get editors, commentators on the radio, labor-group leaders, people of that sort; get them over to the United States and send similar people from the United States to those countries." Among students, where strategic results were normally not expected to show for some time, attention in selection was given to "an individual's prospect of a position of influence in the near future."[65]

The increasing emphasis on propaganda as the objective of cultural activities was highlighted in a frank if undiplomatic memorandum prepared in September, 1951, by two staff members of the Bureau of the Budget in Washington. While the authors were not in a position to formulate policy, their report was praised by Congressman John J. Rooney, chairman of the House appropriations subcommittee dealing with the Department of State, as making "some very, very sensible recommendations." It declared: "The objectives of so-called information and cultural activities are the same; no cultural activity is presently being continued which does not, through its own methods, encourage the unity and strengthening of the free world, increase trust in the United States as a leader of the free world, or expose the evils of communism." The report continued: "Culture for culture's sake has no place in the United States Information and Educational Exchange Program. The value of international cultural interchange is to win respect for the cultural achievements of our free society, where that respect is necessary to inspire cooperation with us in world affairs. In such a situation, cultural activities are an indispensable tool of propaganda."

According to the report, current trends in educational interchange favored activities "which will have immediate effects on the thinking of foreign audiences." Recent developments revealed, among leading foreigners receiving U.S. grants, a marked increase in the number of such persons as government officials, journalists, and labor leaders, who would have an immediate impact on "important target audiences, when they return home."

"Propaganda priorities" applied not only to adult leaders, but also to students. The latter were selected in the light of "the role each candidate can play, on return, to further USIE objectives."[66] The report pointed out that the word "students" was to some degree a misnomer, for in this category during the preceding year only approximately a quarter of those with grants to study here were students in their home country, while the remaining three-fourths were in education, government service, business and industry, journalism, and other occupations.

Turning from exchange of persons to libraries, the report pointed out the recasting of the concept involved in the change of name to "information centers." It stressed the importance of developing "the propaganda sense" in the personnel trained for these centers, which were basically "a propaganda instrument."

The report, in language only slightly more forthright than most official statements, illustrates how completely at this time the concept of reciprocity had been overshadowed by the unilateral emphasis. The idea of give-and-take, of learning from as well as informing the foreign visitor, had almost completely disappeared.

It may be noted that the report was apparently based on an assumption that is somewhat less than realistic concerning the control over foreign individuals invited to visit the United States. While the government with its cooperating private agencies plans where they will travel, and often with whom they will talk, they retain some freedom about their itinerary, and much more about whom they interview. They can observe more or less what they wish. When they return to their home country, they are substantially free—recognizing that they may feel a certain obligation to the United States government or to their own government—to say what they please.

The report also did not concern itself with the possible effect on the foreign visitor of an obviously propaganda-guided experience. Is the experience irksome? Is the aftertaste sweet or sour? If their fellow citizens know that individuals receiving grants are viewed by their hosts as propaganda agents for the United States, do they become objects of suspicion or contempt? Does what they say of the United States become less credible? What is the ultimate effect on the attitude of the people of the receiving country toward the United States?

The "Campaign of Truth" also strengthened tendencies that had appeared earlier to augment the direct participation of the government in transnational cultural activities, in contrast to the part played by private agencies. The government was not only to stimulate, assist, and coordinate as at the start of the program, but increasingly to supplement. Numerous activities were needed, it was argued, for which private organizations could not assume responsibility. The desire of the government to make strategic use of cultural activities led to a reexamination of the role of private agencies in the choice of persons exchanged as well as of books and other cultural activities. Private agencies based their decisions on professional rather than on political factors, and this tended to thwart strategic control. The strategic emphasis, relating as it did to the question of control of policy, also restricted private participation in policy formulation, particularly if advisory commissions and other bodies made up of private citizens were not given full information on the strategic goals of future programs. The two commissions set up by the Smith-Mundt Act were purely advisory in character and had no direct responsibility for the formulation of policy. However, private agencies continued to be largely used for the execution of cultural activities.[67]

Technical Assistance and Economic Aid

The year 1950 witnessed another significant development affecting the cultural program which, however, was not directly related to the "Campaign of Truth." This was the approval by the Congress of the Act for International Development, formally initiating the technical assistance program. Technical assistance has both educational and economic phases, but it involves primarily transmission of knowledge rather than of economic aid in the form of investment capital. Because of its educational emphasis, it must be considered a part of cultural cooperation. In the form of training programs for communicating "know-how," it had been an important element in United States cultural activities from their inception.

The proposal for technical assistance grew out of the work of the Interdepartmental Committee and the Coordinator's Institute of Inter-American Affairs. But its transition to the stage of world affairs was a dramatic one. It illustrated how an idea whose time has come, though originally advanced by a relatively obscure proponent, may carry far when sponsored by a spokesman of prominence.

In the autumn of 1948 a discerning and reflective writer in the Department of State, Benjamin H. Hardy, was doing some preliminary work for the inaugural address President Truman was to deliver on January 21, 1949. He was impressed with the potential significance for the coming years of the earlier work that had been done in Latin America. The fever of the "revolution of rising expectations" was spreading among the underprivileged peoples of all continents. They were beginning to demand for themselves the benefits that science and technology had brought to the peoples of the West. Hardy believed that it would be to the advantage of the United States to cooperate with these disadvantaged peoples in their pursuit of freedom from want, disease, and ignorance.[68] The President liked his ideas.

In Point Four[69] of his inaugural address Mr. Truman said:

More than half the people of the world are living in conditions approaching misery. Their food is inadequate. They are victims of disease. Their economic life is primitive and stagnant. Their poverty is a handicap and a threat both to them and to more prosperous areas.

For the first time in history, humanity possesses the knowledge and the skill to relieve the suffering of these people.

The United States is pre-eminent among nations in the development of industrial and scientific techniques. The material resources which we can afford to use for the assistance of other peoples are limited. But our imponderable resources in technical knowledge are constantly growing and are inexhaustible.

I believe that we should make available to peace-loving peoples the benefits of our store of technical knowledge in order to help them realize their aspirations for a better life. And, in cooperation with other nations, we should foster capital investment in areas needing development.[70]

The President called his proposal "a bold new program." It was new, not in the sense that it was unlike numerous earlier projects for economic development carried out by missionary groups, business enterprises, and the United States government itself in underprivileged countries, but new and also bold in that it committed a major nation to use its resources, as a basic element of its foreign policy, to help not only dependencies or allies but all "peace-loving peoples" to help themselves.

President Truman's inaugural address envisaged technical assistance as being carried forward both by the United States through bilateral projects and by the United Nations agencies through multilateral undertakings. It is significant of the timeliness of the proposal that it resulted in the initiation not only of the Point Four program by the United States, but also of the United Nations Expanded Program of Technical Assistance, and of a more modest program in the Western hemisphere on the part of the Organization of American States. In addition, the United Kingdom and other countries of the British Commonwealth launched the "Colombo Plan" for south and southeast Asia (which has won heavy U.S. support), and France, Norway, and other nations embarked on smaller bilateral programs.[71]

The President spoke before any plan had been worked out to put his idea into action. Only after a debate lasting a year and a half in the public press and in the offices, committee rooms, and halls of government did the Congress approve the Act for International Development,[72] which authorized the technical assistance program. Declaring that "the peoples of the United States and other nations have a common interest in the freedom and in the economic and social progress of all peoples," the Act continued: "Such progress can further the secure growth of democratic ways of life, and expansion of mutually beneficial commerce, the development of international understanding and good will, and the maintenance of peace." Thus along with the cultural objective of international understanding and good will, technical assistance was viewed as furthering the economic objective of increased trade, and the political objectives of democracy and world peace. It was to undergird the efforts of the peoples of the less developed countries to expand their capabilities and their resources "through the cooperative endeavor of all nations to exchange technical knowledge and skills and to encourage the flow of investment capital."

The Congress made it clear that the new program would not be another Marshall Plan for the countries of Asia and Latin America or "a global WPA." Its major emphasis was to be rather on a sharing of technical knowledge than on the provision of capital for economic development. While it was recognized that economic development would require substantial investments of capital, such capital was expected to come from the host countries, from private U.S.

investments that might be made abroad, and from loans on the part of the Export-Import Bank and the International Bank for Reconstruction and Development, related to the United Nations.

For the first year the Congress appropriated $34.5 million for the new program.[73] Within the Department of State a Technical Cooperation Administration (TCA) was set up, to which were transferred the Institute of Inter-American Affairs and the activities carried on by the Interdepartmental Committee. (TCA itself was transferred to the Foreign Operations Administration in September, 1953.) TCA devoted the bulk of its efforts to the traditional areas of agricultural development, public health, and education, although greater attention than formerly was given to increase of industrial productivity and improvement of public administration.

Its training programs were carried on with the cooperation of the Departments of Agriculture, Commerce, Labor, Interior, the Bureau of the Budget, Federal Communications Commission, Federal Security Agency, and the Housing and Home Finance Agency; and, outside the federal government, of universities, industries, and labor unions. Further, some training projects were organized in institutions abroad such as the American University at Beirut and Robert College at Istanbul.[74]

The Economic Cooperation Administration, established in connection with the launching of the Marshall Plan in 1948, had undertaken large overseas operations in both information and training activities. Indeed, the Marshall Plan, with its emphasis on economic recovery for the industrialized nations of Europe, was in a sense an earlier counterpart of "Point Four" technical assistance. At the start, the purpose of the information program of ECA was to explain the nature and motives of American economic assistance and to counter distortions widely broadcast by Soviet propaganda. Later, more emphasis was placed on other objectives, such as the economic integration of free Europe, the increase of agricultural and industrial productivity, wider distribution of the benefits of increased productivity to workers and consumers as well as owners, and encouragement of free enterprise and free labor movements.[75]

The training activities of the Economic Cooperation Administration were started tardily. At the outset the agency accorded scant recognition to the educational phase of the economic assistance enterprise. But it was not long before it was engaged in technical training of the personnel needed to assure continuing development of the agricultural and industrial projects it was supporting. In order to increase the supply of technical, professional, and managerial personnel, the program included training in the host countries with the aid of specialists from the United States, and bringing a considerable number of selected individuals to the United States for training in relation to particular projects. Three kinds of persons were brought from Europe: leading personalities in industry, agriculture, and labor; middle-ranking specialists; and younger persons with a potential for leadership. Members of the first two groups usually came in teams, composed of managers, technicians, and workers, the latter consisting of shop stewards and trade-union leaders. These teams spent several weeks visiting industries for observation and discussion with their American counterparts of methods and procedures for increasing production.

The younger people were organized in "work-study groups." They were recruited from skilled workers in European factories. In the United States, with the cooperation of corporations, labor organizations, and universities, they were provided with on-the-job training in a factory, accompanied by evening discussions on such questions as production methods, management-employee relations, and problems of supervision, the experience lasting up to a year. The program later included visitors from Asia, who were of two types: those of senior rank who came for a brief period to observe production techniques; and those of more junior standing who came for intensive study and learning of particular skills. By fiscal year 1953 the program included approximately 5,600 visitors to the United States, of whom 5,150 were from Europe and some 450 from Asia.[76]

With the outbreak of the Korean conflict in 1950, fear tended to replace hope as the motive for foreign aid. Economic aid and technical assistance were increasingly directed toward expanding the contribution of economic recovery and development to rearmament and resistance to possible Communist aggression. Mutual security became the goal, and economic improvement was viewed primarily as an instrument to that end.

The Economic Cooperation Administration was succeeded by the Mutual Security Agency in 1951. Under the Mutual Security Act of that year, a comparatively small Executive Office agency was established to supervise and coordinate all foreign assistance undertakings, but actual operations were divided among (1) the Defense Department for military assistance, (2) the Mutual Security Agency (MSA) for economic aid, and (3) the Technical Cooperation Administration (TCA) of the Department of State for technical assistance. But the logical division by functions between the last two agencies was shortly replaced by a geographical division, under which MSA took responsibility for operations in Europe and the greater part of southeast Asia, with TCA working in Latin America, the Middle East, south Asia, Burma, and Indonesia.[77]

During the same period the Department of Defense was carrying on certain information activities overseas (not limited to Germany and Japan), which included the Armed Forces radio, certain publications, and specially prepared motion pictures. While the programs of the Armed Forces radio were directed primarily to American servicemen, 90 per cent of their hearers, it was estimated, were local inhabitants. These programs consisted largely of domestic broadcasts, which had been transcribed and "decommercialized." In addition some community relations activities were carried on, designed to ease the inevitable resentment resulting from the presence of foreign troops quartered among another people.

Moreover, under the Mutual Defense Assistance Program, the air force, navy, and army from 1950 to 1959 brought to the United States for technical training approximately 100,000 persons from fifty countries. The primary purpose of this training was to develop essential skills in the use of equipment. But in the case of senior officers concerned with staff work, the experience involved a broad introduction to political and economic as well as military elements in the relations of their countries with the United States.[78]

Cultural Relations in the United Nations Community

The end of the war brought a concentrated effort to develop an institutional framework for the many international cultural interests of the United Nations community. In the development of these

institutions the United States government played a major role. The
United Nations and its many specialized agencies were founded with
a wide variety of responsibilities aside from those intended to meet
political crises and threats of war. Indeed, the bulk of the work of the
specialized agencies and a large proportion of that of the United
Nations itself has been concerned with the advancement and diffu-
sion of knowledge and skills and the application of these to world-
wide problems of health, nutrition, education, social justice, and
general human betterment. They were also concerned with the promotion of mutual understanding by increasing the free flow of information and of knowledge about the peoples and nations that
compose the world community.

The involvement of the United States as a member state in all
these U.N. agencies was an aspect of the growing involvement of
the American people and their government in transnational cultural
activities. It entailed not merely formal ratification of constitutions
and the payment of contributions. It meant the participation of the
American government in the development of the agencies' programs,
the participation of Americans as members of international secretariats, and a growing participation of citizens through specialized
voluntary organizations in agriculture, education, science, public
health, etc., which were concerned with the activities of the international organizations. The process led also to increasing international associations among these voluntary organizations, thus increasing the network of transnational cultural communication. Above
all, it implied the obligation to bring about a rational integration of
national and international, of bilateral and multilateral cultural programs.

During World War II information and cultural activities, including early forms of technical assistance, were carried on as parts of a
total war-time effort, in which the propaganda emphasis gained
mounting strength. With the end of the conflict trends toward distinction reappeared. Support for some cultural activities was extended
by approval of the Fulbright Act and entry of the United States into
the United Nations and its specialized agencies. In contrast, the
value of continuing transnational information activities was for a
time critically questioned. Both programs were viewed as serving

United States foreign policy. They were to advance peace and security by developing understanding and friendly relations with other nations. These relations were to be marked by cooperation and reciprocity. At the same time, the national interests of the United States were to be furthered by promoting true knowledge of the American character and of our purposes and by fostering favorable attitudes abroad.

By 1947 the cold war revealed the necessity for renewed emphasis upon intensive information activities. The Soviet Union was seeking to expand its own power and to weaken the United States by isolating it from its friends and allies. To counter this assault the Congress in 1948 approved the Smith-Mundt Act, authorizing a continuing world-wide information and educational exchange program, with the purpose of improving knowledge of the United States abroad and promoting mutual understanding between the United States and other nations.

The Korean conflict and the 1950 "Campaign of Truth" brought a major expansion of the program and an emphasis on unification, insofar as both cultural activities and information were viewed as propaganda instruments. "Mutual understanding" continued to be a watchword, but was given such unilateral content as to obscure any real top-level concern with reciprocity. Immediate political objectives more and more shaped cultural as well as information programs, and their aims were defined as countering Soviet propaganda attacks, preventing the expansion of Communism, and marshaling cooperation among free world nations. The Point Four program, also initiated in 1950, gave technical assistance a new significance. At first its primary objective was to help the less developed countries. But as it was drawn into closer association with military and economic aid, it was increasingly viewed as an instrument of mutual security to oppose the spread of Communism. In all of these programs, governmental participation progressively assumed a more dominant role, in comparison with that of private agencies.

FOUR

Expansion: 1953-1962

Debate on Character and Objectives

THE EMPHASIS of the "Campaign of Truth" on urgent and unilateral propaganda to combat Communism had by 1953 provoked a reaction. The view had emerged that the character of the whole United States information and cultural program had become "too direct, too shrill, too polemical and, in a sense, too patronizing." Any attempt, it was argued, to manipulate for nationalistic ends the minds and loyalties of our actual and potential friends abroad was contrary to American principles, and was naturally resented by those whose confidence and help we were seeking. This view favored expansion of long-term cultural activities and reduction of radio and press activities to factual reporting in the temper of the BBC. While it recognized that the critical character of the situation created by the cold war demanded a policy of vigorous and careful guidance rather than laissez-faire operation, it held that the program should be honest, calm and moderate, and intellectually mature, and that it should be directed toward the fundamental attitudes and values of foreign peoples.

In contrast, support for the aggressive qualities originally characterizing the "Campaign of Truth" was reinforced by the operations

96

of the McCarthy investigating subcommittee. According to this second view, the overriding threat of Soviet Communism called for the concentration of all efforts and the use of the entire arsenal of psychological weapons against this menace. Indirect and long-term activities that might contribute only remotely to the immediate objective were of distinctly subordinate importance.[1]

Various elements in the first view were reflected in the report of a special Senate committee, which held hearings principally in late 1952 and the spring of 1953 under the chairmanship of Senator J. William Fulbright and later of Senator Bourke B. Hickenlooper.[2] These hearings constituted a major effort to review and appraise the government programs in information and educational exchange. The investigation was searching and critical, but open-minded and fair. It heard a wide array of witnesses—leading figures from motion pictures, radio, newspapers and magazines, book publishers, librarians, educators, and administrators of private exchange activities, as well as numerous officials in the government program. The staff of the committee prepared studies on the United States overseas program, the information program of Great Britain, and the Soviet propaganda program; and drafted summaries of appraisals secured from the heads of U.S. diplomatic missions abroad, from American correspondents overseas, and from business and religious organizations with representatives in foreign countries.[3]

In the conclusions emerging from the investigation, the committee recommended maintenance of a tone in the program worthy of the United States and its citizens; increased cooperation with friendly foreign governments and groups; wider participation by private organizations and individuals; expansion of educational exchanges and overseas libraries; reappraisal of the Voice of America and of the press and publications service; greater stability and continuity in appropriations; and larger autonomy for the activities within the Department of State or establishment of a separate agency.[4] (It was noted that during the preceding five years the program had undergone five major reorganizations and had been headed by five different chiefs.[5])

Another appraisal, instigated by the Eisenhower administration early in 1953, also produced conclusions favoring a shift from the emphases which had been prominent in the "Campaign of Truth."

During the 1952 presidential campaign the foreign information program had become an issue, and General Dwight D. Eisenhower announced that, if elected, he would assure more effective use of psychological measures. In his State of the Union message of February 2, 1953, the new President termed a dynamic information program "essential to the security of the United States and of the other peoples in the community of free nations."[6] He appointed a special President's Committee on International Information Activities under the chairmanship of William H. Jackson to survey and evaluate the government's information and related policies and activities.[7] Its report, presented on June 30, came to the sober conclusion that psychological activities possessed no magic power in themselves. They were effective only in conjunction with other official policies and operations. The report recommended that "American broadcasts and printed materials should concentrate on objective, factual news reporting. . . . The tone and content should be forceful and direct, but a propagandist note should be avoided." (False Soviet charges should, however, be refuted.) The report emphasized the community of beliefs and values shared by the people of the United States with other peoples, and the identity of American goals with those of other peoples. It declared: "The primary and overriding purpose of the information program should be to submit evidence to the peoples of other nations that their own aspirations for freedom, progress, and peace are supported and advanced by the objectives and policies of the United States."[8] Thus bonds of mutual interest were to be stressed. Such a focus, the report implied, would require a shift of emphasis in information activities, where primary attention had been given to the Communist countries—two-thirds of the radio budget going into broadcasts directed behind the Iron and Bamboo Curtains—while presentation to friendly and neutral nations of the United States objectives had taken second place.

However, the menace of international Communism had bred deep and abiding alarm among the American people. Because the menace was double—the cold war without and possible subversion within the United States—what was a healthy fear came in some groups to border on panic and phobia. In contrast to traditional confidence in the strength of American democracy, a negative and defensive attitude had developed. It manifested itself in the restrictive and security-oriented Immigration and Nationality Act of 1952; in apprehension about cultural interchange with Communist countries; in obstructions preventing individuals from entering or leaving the United States to attend international scientific and intellectual meetings—whether non-Communist, private, or governmental. It also manifested itself in a demand for aggressive and unremitting attack on every expression of Communism, both internal and external.

McCarthy Hearings

All these alarms came to a head in the sensational hearings conducted by Senator Joseph R. McCarthy as chairman of the Permanent Subcommittee on Investigations of the Senate Committee on Government Operations. These hearings, initiated in the early days of the Eisenhower administration and concerned with activities of many government agencies, focused attention on certain officials in the government's information and cultural program who were alleged to be ignorant of, or indifferent or favourable to, Communism; and on certain operations of the radio program. They soon turned to the government libraries or information centers abroad and the books they contained. They are worthy of attention because they represented the most flagrant attempt to apply narrow and rigid political criteria to cultural and information activities. They fulfilled the direst prophecies of those who had feared the entry of government into cultural activities.

In connection with the selection of books included in the overseas libraries, Senator McCarthy cast his spotlight, for example, on Howard Fast, some of whose books clearly contained Communist propaganda, on Dashiell Hammett, author of detective stories, and on other writers who invoked the protection of the Fifth Amendment when queried about their alleged Communist views and activities. Louis F. Budenz, a prominent ex-Communist, appeared before the subcommittee and asserted that at least 75 authors whose books were found in the overseas libraries were known to him as Communists. He testified that "a concealed Communist" must have advised placing books by Communist authors in these libraries.[9]

Several years before the start of the McCarthy investigation, careful study had been given to the use in the official information and educational exchange programs not only of books, paintings, musical compositions, and other products by alleged members and sympathizers of the Communist Party, but also of their persons and of news about them. A Department of State directive of August 18, 1949, recalled the American tradition of judging "works of art, literature, science, or scholarship on the basis of merit alone without regard to the political affiliation or leaning of its producers" and the official United States policy on freedom of information opposing discrimination on the basis of race, creed, or political belief. It decided on the principle of "balanced presentation," calling for provision of a factual over-all picture of the cultural phases of American life. Books by American Communists or sympathizers, if of merit in representing characteristic aspects of American life, should not arbitrarily be excluded nor should they be singled out for special stress. They should be presented in the perspective of the total cultural product of the American people, alongside the works of others of comparable stature who might hold different political views.[10]

The Smith-Mundt Act of 1948 (Section 501) had authorized the use of information centers abroad to disseminate information about the United States. These collections of books and publications were therefore in a sense "special purpose" libraries. At the time of the Act's approval, however, one of its sponsors, Senator H. Alexander Smith, had endorsed a statement concerning the overseas libraries adopted by the international relations board of the American Library Association, which advocated that the libraries "offer a broad, honest, nonpropagandistic interpretation of United States life and thought," and that their materials "include all aspects of current life in the United States."[11] This recommendation was substantially followed while the concept of the "full and fair picture" was predominant. With the launching of the "Campaign of Truth" in 1950, propaganda objectives were added to the aims of the libraries, in the sense of making the circulation of American ideas through books a deliberate instrument of foreign policy in the struggle against world Communism.[12]

The question of the inclusion in the overseas libraries of "controversial publications," the loyalty of whose authors had been questioned in some respect, was given special study by the Committee on

Books Abroad, serving as a subcommittee of the Advisory Commission on Educational Exchange.[13] This committee in May, 1952, expressed its belief that "any book whatsoever, of United States origin, which may be of use to the program, should be made available abroad." Its view was endorsed by its parent commission, which added that "it would be deplorable if books expressing views critical of the political and economic situation in this country at any given time were eliminated from the program and the books selected were representative of the views of the Department of State exclusively."[14]

The Committee on Books Abroad supplemented its first statement by advancing six months later the principle that "authorship should not be a criterion for determining whether or not a book is available for USIS libraries abroad"; and recommended that "the content of the book, regardless of authorship, be the criterion which determines its availability for inclusion in USIS libraries."[15] However, Dr. Wilson Compton, then Administrator of the International Information Administration, argued that the character and reputation of the author should be viewed as at least a secondary factor.[16] In consequence a directive of January 30, 1953, while considering content as the primary criterion, held that "materials produced by a person whose ideologies and views are questionable or controversial" should be used only in exceptional cases when the balance was "clearly and strongly in favor" of their effectiveness. Usefulness, therefore, was to be the fundamental consideration. The directive rejected the thesis that a product emanating from an author or creator subject to controversy should be barred irrespective of its content.[17]

But with the onslaught of Senator McCarthy, officials of the new Eisenhower administration precipitately took cover. They did not stop to review the careful and detailed study of the problem during preceding years, or the recommendations made by groups of leading and specially competent private citizens. They did not attempt to weigh the argument that it would be an ostrich policy to attempt to shut off completely knowledge of the objectives of Communism.

On February 13, 1953, the directive of January 30 was rescinded, and six days later, all materials by "Communists, fellow travellers, and so forth" were banned from the libraries and from any use in the program. The vagueness of the language—no authoritative list of Communists and fellow travelers existed, not to mention the difficulty of defining "and so forth"—led to confusion. A few books were burned. Soviet propaganda widely reported what was happening, recalling the Nazi book-burnings. The directive also brought to a halt for a time the Information Media Guaranty Program, guaranteeing dollar exchange for United States books and magazines sent abroad through commercial channels.[18]

Following a wave of protests from within and without government circles in the United States, a new directive was issued on March 17, 1953, largely based on a memorandum issued by Secretary of State Dulles. It dropped the phrase "and so forth," but maintained the ban of all books by Communists and individuals belonging to "Communist fronts." Included were magazines "which often print Communist propaganda." Further, single numbers of "responsible and reputable" magazines which contained "anything detrimental to this country's objectives" were to be removed from circulation and display. Throughout the whole program, a deliberate effort was enjoined to avoid mention of living Communists in press releases, or quotation from them or their works. This directive was supplemented by another on April 23 requiring the banning of books by authors who refused to testify before Congressional committees concerning alleged Communist affiliation.

In the meantime the Advisory Commission on Educational Exchange and its Committee on Books Abroad stood firm on the soundness of their original recommendations. On April 10, 1953, the former declared to the Secretary of State that "an important issue of serious concern to thinking people throughout the entire Nation, and undoubtedly, abroad" had been raised by the "peremptory issuance by the Department of directives which rescinded in full, or in part" those recommendations.[19]

Some aid in stemming the force of the McCarthy attack came when President Eisenhower on June 13 spoke out against book-burning at the baccalaureate service of Dartmouth College. He asked, "How will we defeat communism unless we know what it is? What it teaches—why does it have such an appeal for men?"[20] But the impact of his words was blunted when both he and Secretary Dulles later denied that his statement had any reference to the overseas libraries.

The real turn in the tide apparently came with the approval by the

American Library Association on June 25, 1953, of a manifesto entitled "The Freedom to Read."[21] It asserted: "The freedom to read is essential to our democracy," and called for a return to the American tradition of the free and open mind. An accompanying statement declared that the overseas libraries "do not belong to a Congressional Committee or to the State Department" but to "the whole American people, who are entitled to have them express their highest ideals of responsible freedom." It stressed four points as bases for their integrity and effectiveness:

1. The libraries must express in themselves and their services the ideas of freedom for which they speak.
2. They must provide a service of uncompromising integrity. Their usefulness to the United States rests on the assurance of their users that they are places in which to learn the truth.
3. The Information Administration must be free to use in its libraries what books soever its responsible professional judgement determines are necessary or useful to the provision of such a service. To deny itself the tools it needs to serve the United States for irrelevant reasons of the past associations of authors and in fear of domestic criticism is indefensible.
4. Though no one could justify or would seek to justify the use of the overseas libraries to disseminate material harmful to the United States, it is unworkable to abandon the simple criterion of whether a book is useful to the purpose of the libraries and to substitute elaborate, irrelevant, and offensive schemes of "clearance" of authors.[22]

The forthright statement of the librarians seemed to have clarified the issues as nothing else had. At the same time Senator McCarthy and his unsupported charges had apparently begun to lose public support.[23] The hearings in his controversy with the army were opening. Officials within the information program working with such outside consultants as George Brett of the Macmillan Company and Norman Cousins of the *Saturday Review of Literature* drafted a statement of policy that was issued to the press on July 8 with the approval of Secretary of State Dulles and the President.[24] Its full text was transmitted to the field in a directive of July 21.

The statement declared that the overseas libraries "are in business to advance American democracy, not Communist conspiracy." While these special purpose libraries did not exist to make available "any books that advocate directly or indirectly the destruction of our freedoms and our institutions," books by Communists or by Communist sympathizers might be included "if such authors may have written something which affirmatively serves the ends of democracy." The basic yardstick for selection should be the usefulness of a particular book in a particular situation. Judgment should be based on the book's content without disregarding, however, the reputation of the author. The statement asserted: "Controversial books are of course acceptable and indeed essential, if by 'controversy' we mean honest differences of opinion honestly expressed. . . . Controversy is as American as the varied sounds in the bleachers in a ball park."

A final step was taken when in October, 1953, the overseas libraries were individually given the privilege of choosing the titles they wanted from annotated lists of current books sent out from Washington, none of whose authors, however, were in proscribed categories.

In the struggle over the standards of selection to be applied to the overseas libraries maintained by the United States government, the controversy turned on the writings of Communist and allegedly pro-Communist authors. But at issue was the choice between a rigid ban politically imposed, or the exercise of intelligent and judicious individual judgment in the selection of titles. While the latter principle ultimately prevailed in theory, actual policy made it a general rule to ban all books by known Communists and by persons refusing to testify before Congressional committees concerning their possible Communist affiliation.[25]

The McCarthy investigation, with its misleading statements and exaggerated charges, spread confusion and needless alarm at home, sowed doubts abroad concerning our constancy of purpose and principle, and furnished substantial aid and comfort to hostile Soviet propaganda. But it did not succeed in arresting the trend (faltering at times) away from a narrowly focused opposition to Soviet Communism and toward the use of cultural and information activities in a long-term and cooperative effort to knit together the strength of the free world.

The McCarthy episode, it may also be noted, revealed a striking contrast between the courage, clear thinking, and constancy of the private advisers to the program and the precipitate, ill-judged, and confused actions taken by some of the government officials at high levels. It revealed another contrast also. The Fulbright program with its grants to numerous professors, teachers, and students had also been a prime target for Senator McCarthy. However, after one public hearing on the program, a hearing marked by a sharp defense of the program led by Senator Fulbright, Senator McCarthy retreated and thereafter let the program alone. Its broadly cooperative character and its widespread popular support had made it practically invulnerable to the kind of attack that had been aimed at it.[26]

INFORMATION ACTIVITIES REMOVED FROM THE DEPARTMENT OF STATE

While the debate on the character and objectives of the cultural and information program was in process, another discussion was launched on its most effective location in the United States government. Information activities particularly, involving rapid operations and day-to-day decisions, had not found an entirely hospitable home in the Department of State, with its long-sanctioned procedures of clearance through many offices and its leisurely traditions for the formulation of policy.

In January, 1952, the information and educational exchange activities of the Department of State had been given a semiautonomous status. The purpose of the change was to provide more centralized authority for planning and execution of the program and greater flexibility and independence in management and administration. The "Office of Educational Exchange" was abolished and its constituent divisions for exchange of persons and for libraries and institutes were grouped together with the mass media divisions of the former Office of Information as "media services" of the new "International Information Administration" (IIA). That title, with its lack of any reference to educational activities, was criticized by the Advisory Commission on Educational Exchange, which suggested that it be broadened.[27]

However, this shift in administrative status failed to yield the positive results hoped for by many of the program's supporters. In

January, 1953, the Advisory Commission on Information recommended that the IIA be removed from the Department of State and placed in a new agency of cabinet level. The commission condemned the "lack of enthusiasm and imagination" in the Department of State, the administrative trammels to which the program was subjected, and the "low-level and secondary" position accorded it. It declared that the program had not been granted adequate autonomy for administration of its budget nor adequate control over selection, training, assignment, and management of personnel.[28]

At the same time the influence of the incoming Secretary of State, John Foster Dulles, was thrown into the scales in favor of freeing the Department of State of responsibility for operations, while reasserting its primary leadership in policy. The new administrator of the information and cultural program, Robert L. Johnson, joined Mr. Dulles in urging its transfer out of the Department, arguing that the move would bring "(1) a greater flexibility, (2) a singleness of purpose, (3) a sharper and faster approach, and (4) a better chance to attract highly qualified people."[29] Accordingly, President Eisenhower sent to Congress, on June 1, Reorganization Plan No. 8, which after Congressional hearings came into effect on August 1, establishing the United States Information Agency (USIA). To it were transferred the information and library activities of the Department of State and also the information functions of the Mutual Security Agency. Guidance on policy was to be furnished by the Office of the Assistant Secretary of State for Public Affairs.

In October, 1953, the President, following the recommendations of the Jackson Committee mentioned above, instructed the new agency to explain and interpret to foreign peoples the objectives and policies of the United States, to outline those phases of American life and culture which would facilitate understanding of those policies and objectives, and to depict "imaginatively the correlation between United States policies and the legitimate aspirations of other peoples of the world." It was also to unmask attempts to distort or frustrate U.S. policies.[30]

Thus the objective of the information program was defined as not to seek directly and primarily to "sell" or to develop support abroad for American policies, but rather to show other peoples that American goals and policies were in harmony with their own aspirations. The effort would be to identify the United States with the aims of other peoples. Underlying the mandate to USIA was the assumption that some degree of mutual understanding would be necessary to make clear what were the common interests and common objectives that the United States shared with other countries.

In the meantime, however, another issue had become involved in the question of transfer: whether "educational exchanges," as the term came to be used in the IIA, should accompany information in the shift from the Department of State to USIA. Robert L. Johnson, head of the International Information Administration, had contended in April, 1953, that the exchange of persons was "the hard core" of the entire information program, declaring that these exchanges and the overseas libraries gave information activities "greater strength and greater respectability and greater credibility."[31]

But Senator Fulbright, reflecting the point of view of many educators, led the argument for separating educational exchanges from information and retaining them in the Department of State. He believed that educational exchanges would have a better chance of survival and continuing support if they remained in a permanent agency such as the Department. Further, he held that if the exchanges were linked closely to information activities, they would suffer in the relative attention received from administrators at the top, and would run the risk of being labeled as propaganda, which would undermine their value, and particularly undercut the willingness of distinguished leaders in other countries to cooperate in administration of the Fulbright grants. The senator stressed the impossibility of seeking to make leading educators abroad a part of a national propaganda organization. Such an attempt would inevitably mean the loss of their cooperation. In his view the nonpropagandistic character and the mutual and cooperative factors involved in educational exchanges warranted their separation from the information program.[32]

Senator Fulbright was supported by other interested senators such as Karl E. Mundt, H. Alexander Smith, and Bourke B. Hickenlooper.[33] The latter, as chairman of the special Senate committee previously mentioned, transmitted to President Eisenhower on May 8, 1953, a recommendation from the group urging that educational exchanges be retained in the Department of State.[34]

The members of the Advisory Commission on Educational Exchange also advocated separation of exchanges from information activities. Under the leadership of its chairman, President J. L. Morrill of the University of Minnesota, the group had become concerned about the status of the programs for exchange of persons and for libraries. It believed that long-range cultural objectives were being subordinated to short-range propaganda objectives. It held that these two kinds of objectives were "psychologically different," and while ultimately related, required a different emphasis in their planning and execution.[35]

As a result of these influences, Reorganization Plan No. 8 provided for retention of educational exchanges in the Department of State under the Assistant Secretary for Public Affairs, who was also responsible, among other things, for the Department's participation in Unesco and for policy guidance to USIA. After the resignation of Howland Sargeant, who had held the position in 1952–53, his successors, Mr. Carl McCardle and Mr. Andrew Berding, were primarily charged with the press relations of the Department as well. But no attempt was made to achieve a similar degree of separation for books and libraries, long a companion cultural field to exchange of persons. The McCarthy onslaught had made the libraries a "hot potato," and some partisans of educational exchange may not have wished to invite attack by a link with that activity. Others were puzzled by the ambiguous orientation of the libraries abroad, which has already been described.[36] Accordingly, the libraries were included in USIA, and jurisdiction for advice concerning books and libraries (including the Committee on Books Abroad) was assigned to the Commission on Information, which became the advisory body for the whole of the USIA program. The responsibility of the Commission on Educational Exchange was thenceforth limited to activities relating to exchange of persons and other activities associated therewith, for example, assistance to American-sponsored schools abroad, the Chinese Emergency Aid Program, and all of the cultural activities covered by the Finnish Educational Exchange Act and the India Emergency Food Aid Act.[37]

Had the separation been entirely logical, it would have included the cultural officers who were the agents abroad for exchange of persons. But the Congressional session was almost over; the question of creating a career service for such cultural officers within the regular Foreign Service was an intricate and difficult administrative problem.

In consequence, by what some viewed at the time as a temporary measure, the cultural officers were made responsible by the Department of State to USIA, to which of course were assigned the information officers as well. Thus the distinction between cultural and information activities was not carried out at its most significant point, that of personal contact with foreign peoples. The union of the two in the embassies in effect belied the alleged necessity of separation that had been insisted upon in Washington.

DEVELOPMENTS FAVORING EXPANSION*

NEW EMPHASIS IN INFORMATION PROGRAMS

Cultural activities have experienced increasing recognition and significant growth since 1953. A number of interlocking developments have contributed to this expansion.

One development involved an intensified emphasis on general cultural activities in information programs. Not long after the United States Information Agency had been set up outside the Department of State, Theodore Streibert, its director, initiated efforts to emphasize and expand cultural activities. Its program already included interchanges of books and periodicals, overseas libraries and binational cultural centers, exhibitions, the loan of music and recordings for concerts, broadcasts of American music and other cultural material, and production and circulation of educational and documentary films. In July, 1954, Mr. Streibert dispatched an instruction to all posts abroad, recommending the strengthening of such activities. He recalled the mandate to USIA from President Eisenhower to delineate "important aspects of the life and culture of the people of the United States," and adopted a sweeping definition of culture, viewing it as encompassing "not only scholarly and artistic fields but all significant manifestations and aspirations of the spirit of America, from athletics to political oratory."

These activities were to be emphasized because of their "fundamental importance and lasting quality," and also because they could in his belief influence political attitudes and actions. He referred to

* The developments described in this section are limited generally to those occurring before the end of 1961.

what he termed the Soviet "cultural offensive" and to Soviet propaganda picturing the United States as a nation of materialists, who for
that reason could not be trusted with political leadership. As one step
in the new activity, he had named a Cultural Affairs Adviser and
planned to appoint "cultural representatives" to be sent to foreign
countries.[38]

The Department of State looked askance at this initiative, considering that some of the proposed activities would invade its field of
responsibility for educational exchanges. It held that it should be
responsible for cultural relations, while USIA should limit itself to
so-called cultural information.[39]

Following a joint meeting of the Advisory Commissions on Educational Exchange and on Information, a "task force" representing the
two agencies was appointed to clarify the problem of their respective
fields of responsibility. Its report, presented in April, 1955, recommended a compromise. It did not accept the distinction between cultural relations and cultural information suggested by the Department
of State. Instead it recognized that cultural activities might form a
part of the program of USIA as well as of the Department of State. It
presented a detailed listing of the cultural activities each agency
should properly carry on, but left it open to both of them, depending
on their respective resources, to participate in such enterprises abroad
as the development in universities of American studies, the teaching
of English, and the conduct of seminars, colloquia, and workshops,
together with efforts within the United States to elicit the cooperation of universities and colleges.[40] These findings were more practical
than logical, but they had the virtue of recognizing the complexities
of the *de facto* situation, and they seem to have provided the basis for
a reasonably satisfactory working relationship, which apparently
functioned with less friction in the field than in Washington.

The USIA concern with cultural activities was not short-lived. In
contrast with the "Campaign of Truth," in which short-term information and propaganda objectives had tended to dominate cultural
activities, USIA programs in radio, press, and film, as well as in other
fields, were increasingly directed as time went on toward cultural
goals. International understanding was declared to be the fundamental objective. In 1959 the Advisory Commission on Information
urged that the information program embody characteristics which

traditionally had been claimed for cultural activities. It not only turned away from a propaganda emphasis, recommending that USIA function as a "reliable, honest, non-slanted, authentic reporter of the news"; it stressed the importance of long-range objectives, noting that beliefs and opinions could not be changed overnight. It remarked on the greater interest among other peoples in nonpolitical matters relating to the United States—in American literature, music, and graphic art; in science, education, and economic and social organization. It emphasized reciprocity, pointing out the importance of "a two-way exchange of information and ideas and people," which would correct misconceptions in the United States about other peoples as well as their misconceptions of the American way of life.[41]

Ranking officials of USIA, especially its director, George V. Allen, stressed the increasingly educational character of its program as a contribution to international understanding. In contrast to a declining emphasis on "information in the old sense, the 'propaganda' business and the business of disseminating news," the cultural content of all material was strengthened and expanded. Greater support was given to libraries, university reading rooms, binational cultural centers, art exhibits, and English teaching. Much of the radio and press wireless material had been converted "from the argumentative to the educational and cultural," featuring educational forums and reviews of serious books. The educational approach was termed more effective and more acceptable to foreign peoples. The shift to it from the former "propagandistic" emphasis had resulted not from whim but from a careful evaluation of means and results.[42] As one move to underline the significance of the cultural program, USIA established the policy of assigning an officer experienced in cultural affairs to one of the two top positions in each of its missions abroad.

In his report to the U.S. Advisory Commission on Educational Exchanges in 1961, one of the authors of this volume urged broadening the content of information services through the development of more integrated cultural activities and through more central direction of them under the guidance of the Department of State.

This orientation of information activities has continued under the new administration of Edward R. Murrow. He has been an enthusiastic supporter of the libraries and English language programs.

Under his direction there has been increasing emphasis upon quality and cultural sophistication, in all the activities of the Agency.

Another development grew out of increasing recognition of the importance of education and science to economic development. This drew attention to the relationship between technical assistance and educational exchanges, which had developed within the government as separate programs, though the origin of both was found in the Interdepartmental Committee and the Division of Cultural Relations. With the advent of the Eisenhower administration in 1953, the Foreign Operations Administration (FOA) had absorbed the Mutual Security Agency and the Technical Cooperation Administration (the Department of Defense operating military assistance). In 1955 FOA was replaced by the International Cooperation Administration (ICA), which functioned as a semiindependent unit in the Department of State.

The ICA program, with its emphasis on training for so-called technical occupations relating to economic development, had far outdistanced, in financial support and number of persons involved, the International Educational Exchange Service (IES) of the Department of State. During fiscal year 1956 ICA under its technical cooperation and defense support programs was spending $136 million (including about $16 million for supplies and equipment) for training activities and the exchange of specialized personnel which involved approximately 8,900 persons. The International Educational Exchange Service of the Department of State received for the same year something more than $18 million for exchanges involving close to 5,500 persons.

The expansion of the two programs accentuated concern about their relationship. As early as 1953 Congressional committees had begun to express apprehension about the possibility of duplication and overlapping. In 1955 the Department of State was requested by the Senate and House Appropriations Committees to make a study looking toward the coordination and possible integration of the exchange activities of the two agencies.[44] Dr. J. L. Morrill, President of the University of Minnesota and formerly chairman of the Advisory Commission on Educational Exchanges, was asked to prepare a report on the question, which he presented on May 1, 1956.

The programs of both agencies had to do with the movement of specialized personnel from one country to another, were active in many of the same countries, and were concerned in numerous cases with the same subject matter. But the objectives were defined differently. The purpose of the educational exchange activities of the Department of State, as defined by the Smith-Mundt Act, was to foster better understanding of the United States in other countries and to increase mutual understanding. The purpose of technical cooperation was to help the peoples of the less developed countries, through the sharing of technical knowledge and skills, to expand their resources and to forward their economic development.[45] It was related to the larger context of economic aid.

The two objectives overlapped to a considerable degree, forming what the Morrill Report called a large "grey" area. For example, both agencies were active in the field of education, which plays an important role in the promotion of international understanding and at the same time is an essential factor in economic development. One of ICA's most significant efforts had been the series of contracts made with universities in the United States to aid foreign peoples in specific phases of their economic development. Similarly, overlapping was evident in exchanges relating to public administration, labor, atomic energy, and other fields.

The report noted that ICA in the course of its history had expanded and broadened the meaning of the term "economic development." It stated: "In effect, ICA has so operated . . . as to be concerned with nearly the whole of the body politic of those countries in which it operates programs." Thus its activities impinged on the educational exchange activities of IES and exerted marked influence on the principal objective of IES, the development of international understanding. The presence abroad of some 3,000 American technicians and the introduction into the United States from foreign countries of 6,000 learners, or "participants" as they were called, inevitably increased in those countries knowledge of the United States and of its social and political structure.

IES on its side was charged under the Smith-Mundt Act with the responsibility for rendering technical and other services to foreign peoples, as well as for the interchange of persons. In addition to the academic type of exchange, IES carried on activities designed to meet the technical needs of other countries. According to one estimate, 80 per cent of the foreign students coming to the United States under the IES program could be classified as taking technical training. Thus, according to the report, the two programs "have reached a common point in their growth where the needs they seek to meet cannot be fully met save through an acceptance of their essential unity of purpose and effect."[46]

The report did not, however, consider it wise or feasible to merge the two programs. (The proponents of educational exchange in the Senate and elsewhere feared that such a merger might mean the swallowing up of the broader educational activities sponsored by the Fulbright and Smith-Mundt Acts by the more "practical" and "technical" activities of the larger technical cooperation program.) Each program had its own purpose and function. The report did not favor as a solution the wholesale transfer of undertakings from one agency to the other, or an attempt to redefine in detail their respective spheres of activity. Instead it presented two basic recommendations. First, it urged an "authoritative coordination" of the two programs, to solve the problem of the "grey" area. Second, it called for "an upgrading of U.S. exchange activity in governmental, Congressional, American public and foreign consciousness," thus assuring governmental leadership "in elevating cultural and technical exchange to the level of a major instrument of American influence and assistance in international affairs."[47]

The approach recommended, it was suggested, would combine effectively the resources of the two programs, while maintaining the values and integrity of each. Scholars, students, and others under the educational exchange program travel abroad as private individuals. ICA technicians go overseas as government employees. IES exchanges often involve some degree of reciprocity. ICA activities imply "no contribution in return." ICA represents largely the material side of American life. The IES program brings into play more prominently human and spiritual values.

The report cited on this point a "Joint Statement on United States

Government Participation in Cultural Exchanges" by the National Planning Association which declared:

While American material achievements thus have a positive and creative significance for the whole free world, there are non-material qualities of American culture which are even of greater importance to human progress and which indeed, *are in large measure responsible for our material accomplishments.* These are mainly in the cultural and human relations fields. Our ability to translate into practice our regard for freedom of thought, our belief in the equality of all before the law and in social and economic opportunities, our receptivity to new ideas, and our sense of friendliness and mutual help, are perhaps our most important non-material assets. Today, these qualities yield the social cohesion and voluntary cooperation which make possible the largest functioning democracy in history. These qualities—and their fruits in artistic and intellectual achievements—are not too well recognized abroad, and we can and should make them much more apparent to the peoples of other countries through effective cultural exchange programs and in other ways.[48]

The Department of State accepted the general principles of the Morrill Report, and took some steps toward the more effective coordination recommended. The procedure of "upgrading" the cultural activities program was initiated in December, 1958, by the appointment as Special Assistant to the Secretary of State for Educational and Cultural Relations of Robert H. Thayer, who took over the general direction of the Department's program from Andrew Berding, Assistant Secretary for Public Affairs. The latter has commented on the shift as follows: "But cultural relations are without any doubt sufficiently important unto themselves to warrant their being placed in a separate bureau under the full-time direction of an Assistant Secretary of State."[49] Early in 1960 the U.S. Advisory Commission on Educational Exchanges requested Walter H. C. Laves of Indiana University to review the cultural activities of the U.S. government with a view to increasing their effectiveness. The integration in both policy and operations of educational exchanges and technical assistance was one of the major recommendations in the Laves Report.[49a]

Thayer was succeeded in 1961 by Philip H. Coombs, and in 1962 by Lucius Battle with the title of Assistant Secretary of State for

Educational and Cultural Affairs. Both Coombs and Battle served as head of the Bureau of Educational and Cultural Affairs, which brought together the principal elements in the Department concerned with cultural activities.[50]

CONGRESSIONAL ACTION ON EDUCATIONAL EXCHANGES

The expansion of cultural activities has also been encouraged by Congressional approval of new legislation on educational and cultural exchanges, to supplement the Fulbright and Smith-Mundt Acts and to pull together various existing pieces of legislation into an integrated whole. A considerable amount of financial support for such exchanges already derived, in fact, from a series of separate legislative acts dating back to the end of World War II. Under the "G.I. Bills" 19,000 veterans of World War II and (by 1960) more than 6,000 veterans of the Korean conflict were given opportunity to study abroad.[51] While this legislation concerned only American citizens, other laws were designed for the benefit of individual foreign countries. The Philippine Rehabilitation Act of 1946 (P.L. 370, 79th Cong., 2d sess., 60 Stat. 128 [1946] as amended) provided for training in the United States of some 850 Philippine citizens in scientific, technical, and public-service fields. In 1949 the Finnish Educational Exchange Act sponsored by Senator H. Alexander Smith allocated part of the annual payments by Finland on its post-World-War-I reconstruction loan to the interchange of students, teachers, and technicians, and the exchange of books and educational equipment with that country (P.L. 265, 81st Cong.). In 1950 the Iranian Trust Fund (an indemnity of $110,000 paid by Iran in 1924 and 1925) was assigned to the education of Iranian students in the United States (P.L. 861, 81st Cong.).

The conquest of the Chinese mainland by the Communists cut off cultural interchange between the United States and that area. This led to the setting up of a Chinese Emergency Aid Program for students and scholars, administered by the Department of State. It was financed by the Economic Cooperation Administration, by funds authorized by the Foreign Appropriations Act of 1950 (P.L. 327, 81st Cong.), and by the China Area Aid Act of 1950 (Title II of P.L. 535, 81st Cong.). These sources made it possible to assist some

3,500 Chinese students and about 100 scholars stranded in the United States to finish their educational programs, and to bring to the United States for short periods of study two score Chinese students and scholars from various areas of the Far East. Following the aggression against the Republic of Korea in 1950, similar aid was authorized for a small number of Korean students stranded in the United States (P.L. 165, 82d Cong.). (The program for assistance to China and Korea came to an end in 1955.) In 1951 a provision of the India Emergency Food Aid Act, sponsored by Senator Karl E. Mundt, authorized use of the interest payments (not to exceed $5 million) for educational exchanges similar to those with Finland (P.L. 48, 82d Cong.). In 1954 an agreement with Ireland provided for the use of approximately 500,000 Irish pounds for scholarship exchange with that country (P.L. 665, 83d Cong.).[52]

Legislation of a somewhat different character in 1948 (P.L. 402, 80th Cong., as amended) authorized the Information Media Guaranty Program. This program made possible the commercial sale of American books, periodicals, and motion pictures to citizens of foreign countries that were short on dollar exchange. The program guaranteed the exporting publisher payment in dollars in return for the foreign currencies he had received from his foreign customers. During the period 1948–59 this legislation made possible the sale abroad of $40 million worth of these materials in eighteen foreign countries at a net cost of approximately $13 million, this latter figure representing the loss incurred when the foreign currencies were resold to replenish the supply of dollars.[53]

After 1953 new legislation of prime importance was approved along two lines. One concerned the dwindling supply of authorized foreign currencies, which threatened to terminate the Fulbright program in certain countries. The sources of foreign currency were broadened under the Mutual Security Acts of 1954 and 1956, notably by the Agricultural Trade Development and Assistance Act of 1954 (P.L. 480, 83d Cong., as amended), which authorized the use of proceeds from the sale of surplus agricultural commodities for educational exchanges, and later also for the translation, publication, and distribution of books and periodicals abroad, for assistance to American-sponsored schools, libraries, and community centers, and for promotion of "American studies" in foreign countries.

By 1962 these various pieces of legislation enabled 44 countries to participate in the Fulbright program—countries situated in all major areas of the world outside the Communist bloc.

The second major legislative measure was the International Cultural Exchange and Trade Fair Participation Act of 1956 (P.L. 860, 84th Cong.). This act authorized on a continuing basis appropriations for a program originally initiated in 1954 as the result of a special request by President Eisenhower. In the field of cultural interchange, it facilitated the appearance abroad of American musicians, dramatic companies, and sport groups which will be discussed below.

The question of appropriations for educational exchanges during the period under review brought forth expressions of widespread public support, and, in the Congress, sharply contrasting attitudes in the Senate and the House of Representatives.[54] When the 1955 appropriation for such exchanges was slashed by the House from $15 million to $9 million, full restoration of the cut was urged before the Senate Appropriations Committee by Vice-President Nixon, Senators Homer E. Capehart, J. William Fulbright, Karl E. Mundt, and Edward J. Thye, as well as by Congressman Walter Judd. Favorable testimony and communications were presented by a broad battery of national organizations, including the American Association of University Women, American Council on Education, American Federation of Teachers, National Education Association, and National Student Association, as well as by the American Federation of Labor, American Veterans Committee, General Federation of Women's Clubs, National Catholic Welfare Council, National Council of Jewish Women, National Council of Negro Women, National Farmers Union, and the American Chambers of Commerce of Brazil.[55] The entire cut was restored. Similarly, when the House cut the appropriation for 1956 from $22 million to $12 million, widespread protest was raised.[56]

The negative actions taken by the House were in large part a reflection of the attitude of Congressman John J. Rooney, chairman of the appropriations subcommittee for the Department of State, and certain of his colleagues. The subcommittee's crippling slash of the 1956 appropriation was defended on the floor by only one Representative—outside of its own membership—while 16 Congressmen of both parties spoke out against the cut and in support of the program. A motion for restoration, however, failed to muster the necessary majority.[57]

When the Department of State reduced its request for educational exchange in the 1957 appropriation from $22 million for the previous year to $20 million, it was challenged by Senator Fulbright. In answer to its defense that the administration had imposed a budget ceiling, the Senator pointed out that USIA had been permitted to ask for a $50 million increase. Further, the Advisory Commission on Educational Exchange had recommended a figure of $31 million.[58] Senator Fulbright declared: ". . . the administration is completely wrong in decreasing this very modest exchange program, because it has a special influence, I think, in many countries which have long felt that this country has no appreciation of the intellectual activities of mankind or their cultural achievements." He concluded, "I am not satisfied with the evaluation of this program by the Department of State, and I do not intend to be satisfied with it." The Department had recommended a decrease in "the only program that is related to the cultural activities of civilized human beings."[59]

As one move to redress the situation, the Committee on Foreign Relations, noting that "There is a serious question whether a proper balance is being maintained" between the information and educational exchange programs, recommended as one amendment to the Smith-Mundt Act permission to the President to transfer 10 per cent of the funds for information to educational exchange.[60]

For the 1959 appropriation for educational exchanges, the Senate Appropriations Committee, largely on the initiative of Senators J. William Fulbright and Lyndon B. Johnson, recommended an increase of $10 million over the amount of $20.8 million requested by the Department of State and approved by the House Appropriations Committee.[61] However, the final amount agreed on by both House and Senate was $22.8 million.

The legislation dealing with cultural activities approved by the Congress had been impressive in its range and variety. But it had added up to a mass of often unrelated acts. It had been a patchwork of pieces that did not fit together to make a unified picture. Serious gaps existed—for instance, the limitation of support for the Fulbright program and certain other activities to countries where counterpart funds from surplus war stocks or surplus agricultural products became available. There was urgent need to codify and amplify the existing mass of legislation. On March 2, 1961, Senator Fulbright introduced a comprehensive bill (S. 1154) designed to achieve these ends for a wide range of cultural activities, not including, however, educational programs involved in technical assistance. As a participant in planning the new legislation, in testimony before the Senate and House Committees as well as in his report to the Advisory Commission on Educational Exchanges, Laves urged that a much closer relationship be assured between these two aspects of U.S. cultural activities abroad. A companion bill (H.R. 8666) was introduced by Representative Hays on August 14. The final Fulbright-Hays Act was passed by Congress on September 16 and signed by President Kennedy on September 21. The size of the Congressional vote (Senate 79–53; House 378–32) is eloquent testimony of the support which this part of the U.S. cultural relations program now enjoys.

A detailed commentary by the Executive Secretary of the Conference Board of Associated Research Councils, Francis A. Young, provides excellent summaries of the most significant changes brought about by the Act.[62]

The statement of purpose in the Act succeeds much better than does previous legislation in harmonizing educational and political objectives. It makes clear that the ultimate purpose of the Act is political in the broadest and best sense, namely "to assist in the development of friendly, sympathetic and peaceful relations between the United States and the other countries of the world." But this basically political objective is closely linked with the educational and humanitarian ideal by specification in the statement of purpose that the legislation seeks "to promote international cooperation for educational and cultural advancement" and by a clear stress upon the mutuality of the programs. The Act itself is to be known as the Mutual Educational and Cultural Exchange Act, and the old phrase "to promote a better understanding of the United States in other countries" becomes in the new Act "to increase mutual understanding between the people of the United States and the people of other countries."

To the kinds of cultural activities previously authorized by various pieces of legislation are added U.S. and foreign representation at international nongovernmental educational and scientific meetings held under American auspices in or outside the United States and independent research into problems of educational and cultural exchange.

Financial support is made much more flexible by permitting use of funds made available under the Act for any of the programs authorized and permits exchanges to be arranged on the basis of grants, contracts, or otherwise through institutions as well as on an individual basis. More than this,

not only may the President enter into multilateral as well as bilateral agreements, but these agreements may cover all aspects of educational and cultural relations, and not merely the kind of exchanges included in the limited Fulbright agreements of the past. There is a similar broadening of the potential role of the binational foundations or commissions which have heretofore administered the Fulbright program abroad. These agencies may now be used for the overseas administration for any of the programs conducted under the Act. The way is also open for cooperating foreign countries to share in the cost of the programs, especially in the use of their own currencies and in the support of their own grantees. The result is not only to increase and strengthen the elements of mutuality in the program but also to widen the area of activity in which the educational community shares responsibility with the government.

[Furthermore] . . . the fiscal provisions of the Act contain some important new authority. Appropriations remain available until expended, thus permitting the assured financing of particular projects over a period of years. There are also no legal limits, other than those imposed by appropriations, on the annual size of country programs, thus removing the old ceiling of $1,000,000 contained in the earlier Fulbright Act. This is a matter of some practical consequence in the case of a country like India, for which very large reserves of foreign currencies are available. Another interesting provision is that the President may transfer from one government department to another funds appropriated in furthering the purposes of the Act. This provides a financial mechanism for closer interdepartmental coordination of related programs; it would be a miracle of the bureaucracy however if it should become extensively used.[63]

Of particular importance is authorization for importing foreign cultural presentations on a nonprofit basis as well as the exportation of American cultural presentations.

The Act gives the President wider discretion in assigning administrative responsibility for the various kinds of activities included under the Act.

The Act provides many administrative improvements relating to the operation of exchange programs. There are also some modifications in the functions of the three advisory boards and there are major modifications in immigration regulations affecting exchangees.

NEW EMPHASIS ON THE ARTS

Another development contributing to the expansion of cultural activities was the enlistment of the arts in the United States cultural program. Aside from certain war-time projects in Latin America supported by the Coordinator of Inter-American Affairs, the arts had been treated as a stepchild. Had it not been for the challenge of Soviet cultural competition, the value of the arts as an expression of the American spirit might have continued to go largely unrecognized.

An incident in 1946 had a decisive effect in relegating them to the sidelines. In that year the Department of State sponsored two exhibitions of contemporary American painting to tour Europe and Latin America. The pictures had won praise from the critics at a showing in the Metropolitan Museum of New York City. But their "advanced" character was attacked by Congressmen and by conservatives outside government circles. In consequence the exhibitions were called back, and Secretary Marshall announced that the Department would buy no more examples of American painting.

The hostile attitude in the Congress led to disregard and neglect of the fine arts in general and to a specific injunction against government-financed exhibitions of paintings that had not received individual, prior approval from the legislative body.[64]

The situation in Germany was an exception to the general rule. When in 1949 the cultural program in West Germany was transferred to the Department of State from the army, the request for appropriations included the term "art." The Department dispatched several exhibitions to Germany and in addition government funds were used to send American musical and dramatic productions to the Berlin Festivals of 1951, 1952, and 1953, including *Oklahoma, Porgy and Bess, Medea* with Judith Anderson, the Juilliard String Quartet, and two ballet companies.[65] Support by public-spirited private citizens made it possible to present to other European countries a number of productions in the field of music and drama.

But private efforts were at best fragmentary and sporadic and by the mid-fifties opinion was growing that the government should assume a larger share of the financial burden. The Soviet cultural offensive continued with increasing momentum. Too many of the leaders of thought and opinion in other countries still cherished the conviction that "Americans live in a cultural wasteland, peopled only with gadgets and frankfurters and atom bombs."[66]

In consequence, President Eisenhower sought and was given in 1954 an Emergency Fund of $5 million annually for musical and dramatic presentations abroad and for United States participation in international trade fairs.[67] Two years later the program was made permanent by Congressional enactment of the International Cultural Exchange and Trade Fair Participation Act of 1956 referred to above (p. 118). Under this legislation government funds were to supplement the fullest possible private support—income derived from private contributions in the United States as well as that from box-office receipts for performances overseas. An Advisory Committee on the Arts was established to advise the Secretary of State regarding programs.

By June, 1962, 24 dance projects, 21 theater projects, 63 sports projects, and over 100 musical projects had been carried out in more than a hundred countries. The program made possible appearances abroad of almost a dozen leading American symphony orchestras; numerous choral groups and ballet troupes; dramatic companies presenting such plays as Eugene O'Neill's *Long Day's Journey into Night* and Thornton Wilder's *Skin of our Teeth;* and such individual performers as Marian Anderson, William Warfield, Rudolph Serkin, and Isaac Stern.

American jazz, which on its own momentum had won its way to world-wide recognition, entered the program in 1956 as the result of many field requests, and was welcomed by immense audiences, in which students and other young people were prominent. Jazz groups sent on tour included those of Louis Armstrong, Dave Brubeck, Benny Goodman, Sauter-Finegan, and Jack Teagarden.[68]

The effects of the cultural presentations program went far beyond the persons attending the performances. Television and radio broadcasts reached vast audiences exceeding the capacity of the largest theater or concert hall. Showings of motion pictures of the performances expanded and continued the impact of the tours. Reviews of the events in the local press were seen by millions of readers.

While the program emphasized primarily professional performers of the highest caliber, a small number of amateur and student groups were also included, such as the Westminster and Howard University choirs and theater groups from several universities. Groups of this character made a special appeal to university audiences and served to build a youth-to-youth relationship.

Sports figured in the President's Special International Program from the start, calling forth an interest that cut across all economic and social levels and almost all age groups. Outstanding individual athletes and baseball, soccer, tennis, and swimming teams put on exhibitions. Athletic competition with the Soviet Union rose sharply as a result of the bilateral agreement signed in 1958.

These presentations, both artistic and athletic, reflected varied aspects of American life. In a number of groups Negroes and whites lived and traveled together, and performed side by side. Off stage as well as on, the American performers showed themselves approachable, friendly, and helpful. They offered special performances for students and for children. They sought contact with their colleagues in the host countries, sharing knowledge and ideas.

In the field of the visual arts, private agencies in the United States have played a more prominent and decisive role than government bodies. Among the latter, the United States Information Agency, which at its establishment was given the responsibility for exhibitions, has been most active in showing American art abroad. It has circulated exhibitions, not only of paintings, but of prints and drawings, American architecture, Indian arts and crafts, and the widely-shown "Family of Man," a collection of photographs by Edward Steichen, depicting the basic human qualities and practices of mankind in all parts of the world. USIA has frequently enlisted private individuals or organizations on a contract basis to prepare exhibitions for showing in foreign countries.

While USIA has regarded domestic exhibition of foreign art as beyond the bounds of its responsibility, the Smithsonian Institution has been active in sponsoring such showings. Among these exhibitions have been showings of Austrian drawings and prints, Chinese landscape paintings, and collections of abstract paintings by contemporary artists from both Canada and Japan. Shows in the applied arts have presented Burmese embroideries, Danish silver, contemporary Indian crafts, Italian industrial design, Swedish textiles, and collections of photographs on postwar Brazilian, Finnish, and German architecture.[69]

The program in music, ballet, and theater, so far as government participation is concerned, has been a one-way street. Official funds have gone to "exporting" American attractions abroad, none to "importing" foreign artists into the United States. But private impresarios have redressed the balance to a degree, by bringing French and British theater groups and dance companies from Bali, India, Japan, and the Soviet Union—to mention only a few—to this country. In addition, the American performers going abroad have frequently shown active interest in learning about and learning from the national arts of the people they are visiting.

The official objectives of activities in the arts have been to counteract Soviet influence and propaganda, and to correct and humanize the image of the American people held by other peoples, thus to develop a more rounded understanding of the United States, and greater confidence in its leadership in world affairs. According to this view the United States is well known abroad for its technological skills, its fabulous capacity for mass production and consumption, its extension to a large majority of its people of well-being and what passes for luxury in other societies. But other peoples have been disposed to look down on the United States as a nation concerned only with the creation of material wealth and with the satisfactions provided by creature comforts and ingenious gadgets. If they were to look upon Americans as capable of understanding and sharing the finest achievements and values mankind has created, it was necessary to correct the distorted image so widely held.

Private activities have tended to emphasize rather the reciprocal values of artistic interchange, which may stimulate the development of the arts themselves and broaden and deepen the appreciation of the arts by the general public. Presentations of music and drama as well as of the visual arts have been cordially received. The visits of artists of the first rank have often been interpreted as a mark of respect and esteem. One newspaper editor remarked, "If this is cultural imperialism, let us have more ot it."

A companion activity to the cultural and athletic exchanges under the President's Special International Program has been United States participation in international trade fairs. In this field also the Soviet Union has been expanding its activities. Together with the other countries of the Communist bloc, it increased its participation from 15 fairs in 1950–51 combined to 93 in 1956. While the trade fairs have the expansion of commerce as their primary objective, the American exhibits necessarily present a vivid and variegated picture of certain aspects of American life. They are purveyors of information, knowledge, and perhaps the beginnings of understanding. Among the exhibits shown have been a one-room air-conditioned school, an American-type children's playground, a well-stocked American bookstore, and a medium-priced, one-floor suburban residence, fully equipped and furnished.

THE CHALLENGE OF SOVIET COMPETITION

Another development that had an important bearing upon the expansion of cultural activities was the changing attitude of the Soviet Union toward cultural exchanges with the West. The policy of coolness toward cultural interchange which had prevailed substantially since the latter half of the 1930s, and which warmed up during World War II only to freeze again by 1947, had been definitely modified by 1953, and even to some extent before that time. By 1950 the Soviet Union began to admit some students from non-Communist countries and a little later to dispatch some of its most prominent musical and ballet performers as well as certain motion pictures to participate in international festivals and competitions.

But it was not until the death of Stalin in 1953 that the U.S.S.R. initiated a widespread endeavor to use cultural activities as a significant element in its relations with non-Communist countries. From 1953 to 1955 the number of delegations entering and leaving the country (the U.S.S.R. computes this movement by delegations rather than by individuals) increased threefold. In the latter year two-thirds of the total was with countries outside the Communist orbit.[70]

Scientists lecturing to scholarly audiences, musicians playing in concert halls, and football and other athletic teams performing in stadia were all parts of the same offensive to impress foreign peoples with a favorable picture of life in the Soviet Union and with the cultural fruits of Communist society. Soviet books were actively flooding into many of the countries of Asia. Often handsomely produced but subsidized to sell at low prices, they ranged from literary classics and elegantly illustrated books on art to children's story books, from volumes by Marx, Engels, and Lenin for intellectuals to low-cost propaganda pamphlets for the general public. The Soviet Union began a foreign aid program in 1954. Linked with this was a growing program of technical assistance for the less developed countries. By 1959 some 4,700 Communist-bloc technicians were providing aid to non-Communist countries (the United States had 6,000 technicians abroad at this time), and approximately the same number of students from these countries had gone for training to the Iron Curtain countries.[71]

The Soviet Union was disposed not only to press cultural rivalry with the United States in the industrialized countries of Europe and the less developed countries of other continents, but also to embark on cultural interchange with the United States itself, if such interchange could redound to its benefit. At the same time the United States was eager to pierce the Iron Curtain and to establish direct contacts with the Soviet people.

This was one of the principal proposals at the summit conference in 1955. However, nothing came of discussions on the matter at the succeeding meeting of the foreign ministers later the same year. Some specific exchange projects were nonetheless carried out at that time, and negotiations that began in the fall of 1957 resulted in the approval of a bilateral U.S.–U.S.S.R. cultural agreement in January, 1958, to run for two years. It provided for a wide range of exchanges: industrial and agricultural delegations; scientists, artists, and writers; symphony orchestras and ballet companies; athletic groups; and a small number of students and professors—all of which eventually totaled about 2,000 individuals on each side—as well as motion pictures, exhibits, and a varied array of publications. In the summer of 1959 an exhibition of American life with emphasis on science and art was presented in Moscow's Sokolniki Park and a similar Soviet exhibition in New York City's Coliseum. The results of the agreement were sufficiently satisfactory to both parties to be continued for a second two-year period during 1960–61 and again for the two-year period 1962–63.

Substantial use has been made of the opportunities under the modified Soviet policy and the three cultural exchange agreements of 1958, 1959, and 1962. During the period January 1, 1958, to December 31, 1961,[72] some 303 projects known to the State Department were undertaken by the United States, taking 3,797 Americans to the Soviet Union. This does not include American tourists going to the U.S.S.R., estimated at about 3,500 during the four-year period. Some 318 Soviet projects brought 3,105 Soviet citizens to the United States and, in addition, there were an estimated 1,200 Soviet tourists in this country.

Most of the scientific, educational, and other scholarly exchanges were arranged under the three governmental agreements or the supplementary agreement involving the National Academy of Sciences of the United States, the American Council of Learned Societies, and the Inter-University Committee on Travel Grants. These exchanges included students, professors, and research workers. In the field of the natural sciences were included projects for specialists in various fields to attend conferences and to visit research institutions.

During 1961 industrial delegations were exchanged in fields such as petroleum, railroads, cement, highways, and civil air transport. Agricultural exchanges involved delegations in food processing, agricultural information, soil research, chemical fertilizer, and livestock production. Medical exchanges included delegations for conferences on topics such as cancer and heart disease, and for individual research. A number of performing arts exchanges have been included over these three years.

There have been exchanges of motion pictures, radio and television programs, of the two governmental publications, *Amerika* and *USSR*, and of exhibits such as those on plastics, transportation, and medicine sent by the United States and some on children's books, medicine, and children's arts sent by the U.S.S.R.

There has been an increasing number of exchanges arranged directly by universities and other institutions. These have been generally in the areas of science and scholarly research, but there have also been some for youth groups, track, tennis, and other athletic teams, and for music and ballet.

One of the most interesting U.S. cultural activities has developed in the setting of the U.S.–U.S.S.R. agreements. The Inter-University Committee on Travel Grants was founded by a group of universities (now totaling 35) to increase knowledge in the United States about the Soviet Union. Their initiative came from a conviction that upon the universities rested a major responsibility in our kind of society to increase the educational efforts toward this end. Within the terms of the intergovernmental cultural exchange agreements, and financially supported by foundation, government, and university funds, the Inter-University Committee deals directly with the Soviet Ministry of Higher Education. It arranges with the ministry for the annual program of exchanges of students and scholars and is responsible for the selection of Americans and approval of Soviet names proposed for exchanges. It assists in the placement of exchangees at universities in the two countries. It negotiates directly with the ministry over basic issues such as access to libraries and archives. In spite of the inherent difficulties due to different educational systems, to immensely complicated placement problems, to the position of an inter-university committee vis-à-vis a powerful governmental bureaucracy, and to the inevitably different objectives of the American universities and the Soviet Ministry of Education, this method of handling the exchanges has been highly useful. It has permitted on the American side the development of a system of selection and administration consistent with highest academic standards and the greatest possible separation of the exchange system from the day-to-day political tensions between the two governments. It has permitted flexibility and experimentation in developing relations with the Soviet government, relatively free from preoccupation with the prestige position of the United States or other immediate political objectives. It has placed the American exchangees outside the immediate official family of the U.S. Embassy in Moscow, emphasizing thereby the primarily scholarly interests of the American universities. Finally, and perhaps most importantly, it permits Soviet visitors sponsored by the Committee under the program to observe the vitality, quality, and nonpolitical character of the American academic community.

DEMANDS FOR HELP FROM THE LESS DEVELOPED COUNTRIES

The increasingly insistent demands of the less developed countries for technical assistance represented another pressure for the expansion of cultural activities after 1953. These countries had been pressing for recognition of their need for social as well as for economic development. They were increasingly restive over the heavy emphasis upon military support and purely economic growth found in much U.S. assistance during the cold war. A growing opinion in the United States and also in other industrialized countries was stressing the need for a shift in emphasis. Criticism was increasing that the prevailing policy was too narrow in limiting international loans to projects promising increased productivity and output of goods, and excluding those for other than purely economic purposes.

A clear shift in United States policy became evident in July, 1960, when President Eisenhower announced a "Social Development Plan" for Latin America. In August the Congress authorized a $500 million fund for this purpose. In September an inter-American economic conference held in Colombia adopted the Act of Bogota. The Act called for active measures for stimulation of social development, including land reform, housing, education, and health; a special fund for social development to be administered primarily by a new Inter-American Development Bank; additional measures for economic development; and multilateral cooperation for social as well as economic progress.[73] Strongly featured was the importance of self-help. Thus educational services through technical assistance, which previously had been assigned a narrowly construed and peripheral place in the over-all enterprise for economic aid, were given a centrally recognized role. This emphasis was spelled out in proposals for mass education to eradicate illiteracy, rural and vocational education, and also secondary and higher education. Thus a conception of assistance as broad, almost, as the full range of cultural activities was emerging in statements of policy even though programs and especially appropriations still reflected narrow categories that had developed during the previous decade—categories that continue to impose organizational patterns and administrative procedures that are at variance with the character of national needs.[74]

President Kennedy attempted a more comprehensive approach to development assistance in his proposal to Congress for a new Act for International Development[75] and in his invitation to the American nations to join in an Alliance for Progress.[76] This approach is reflected in language that emphasizes the need for involvement of local national resources in the planning and execution of aid programs, the need for long-term planning by the underdeveloped countries, the need for a cooperative approach by the United States together with other free world countries and the United Nations, and the need for social progress within the underdeveloped countries that wish to receive U.S. assistance. The policy language increasingly uses the "development of human resources" instead of merely "economic development," and hence encourages greater emphasis upon educational development at all levels as well as strictly technical education. It also emphasizes the important contribution to political understanding that may result from imaginative programs and high quality in administration.[77]

The more comprehensive character of assistance to underdeveloped countries means that many functions such as English-language teaching, educational exchanges, and libraries, undertaken originally for quite different reasons, now are necessary parts of the total assistance effort demanded by national policy. Categories of functions assigned to various governmental agencies have in many instances become outmoded, and it is too early, as of 1962, to determine whether the new policy language will in fact be translated into necessary new kinds of operations.

PEOPLE-TO-PEOPLE MOVEMENT

In May, 1956, speaking at Baylor University in Texas, President Eisenhower called for more sympathetic understanding among the peoples of the world. Such understanding, he held, was essential to prosperity and peace. He suggested more active participation by private individuals and groups in relations with other peoples. He urged "a voluntary effort in people-to-people partnership" as a fruitful corollary to what the government itself was doing.[78]

The President followed up his Baylor talk by calling together in September a group of several score leaders of American business, professions, and voluntary organizations in numerous fields. At this White House Conference he announced: "If we are going to take advantage of the assumption that all people want peace, then the problem is for people to get together, and to lead governments—if necessary, to evade governments. . . ." Looking at his hearers, he remarked, "Here are people that we hope will lead us."[79] Thus the People-to-People program was launched.

The next step inevitably was to organize committees, 41 of them. They brought together industrialists, publishers, educators, advertising men, scientists, Hollywood entertainers, cartoonists, labor leaders, physicians, radio, television, and motion picture executives, writers, musicians, artists, leaders of farm, fraternal, religious, veterans', women's, and youth groups, and hobbyists of manifold variety. Each group was to work out its own channel for international communication. Ideas were marshaled and paraded, some of them time-worn, others original and at times bizarre. William Faulkner, in an effort to stimulate the thinking of his fellow writers, proposed among other suggestions to "anaesthetize, for one year, American vocal cords;" to "abolish, for one year, American passports;" and to bring to the United States 10,000 persons, preferably Communists, "and let them see America as it is.[80]

Half of the committees had in common one practical idea—they needed money. Various schemes were tried, all disappointing. Foundations were willing to favor these new additions to the variegated flora of American organizations, despite or perhaps because of the hothouse atmosphere of official favor in which they had germinated. The new vegetation in some cases was overrunning the vested interests of private agencies which had long been at work. However, some new activities blossomed. For example, leaflets were prepared to give to the foreign-bound American traveler when his plane took off or his ship left dock. Their theme was "Make a friend this trip." But when the fanfare and the organizational busy work came to an end, much of the new growth withered away.

But something remained and something continued, thanks in part to the constant assistance provided to numerous efforts by USIA's Office of Private Cooperation. It extended modest grants to approximately 12 of the committees to cover administrative expenses. In many cases the main effect of the campaign was to give a new push to voluntary activities that had been growing for some time. The movement encouraged American towns and cities to affiliate with municipalities abroad, American corporations and business firms operating overseas to cultivate better community relations, American individuals to write letters, contribute books, and send past issues of magazines to individuals in foreign countries and to provide home and community hospitality to foreigners visiting the United States, numerous and varied organizations to adopt overseas projects or to engage in exchanges with their corresponding associations abroad. One major project was the dispatch in 1960 of the S.S. *Hope,* outfitted as a clinic-hospital, on a two-year cruise, with the first stop in Indonesia. It was made possible by contributions, in addition to some government funds, from the drug, food, and oil industries, from many private groups and individuals, and by volunteer aid from numerous physicians. A similar trip of the S.S. *Hope* was under way in 1962, this time to South America.

Although the activities of the People-to-People movement have been spotty, and sometimes superficial and sentimental, they have led many persons and groups in the United States to widen their horizons and to make foreign contacts that were helpful in both directions. But in serious and sustained impact, they have fallen short of the numerous long-term programs carried on by foundations and by educational, scholarly, religious, and industrial groups and organizations.

EAST-WEST CENTER IN HONOLULU

A unique effort to combine many kinds of cultural activities in the context of a program designed to develop and strengthen relations between Western and non-Western countries was authorized in the establishment by Congress of a Center for Cultural and Technical Interchange between East and West at the University of Hawaii. The Center came into being on October 25, 1960, with the help of a grant-in-aid made by the Department of State to the university. Congress is to continue annual appropriations for support of the Center.

The significance of this action lies not merely in the commitment of direct governmental support[81] for this kind of academic institution, but also in the focus of the Center, which combines the promotion of understanding through educational exchanges, teaching, study, and research; the deliberate effort to reach not only established persons but promising potential leaders; and insistence that the educational experiences and research at the Center shall be designed to advance the human welfare of the developing countries. In many respects the Center reflects in an academic setting the convergence of most of the different elements in U.S. transnational cultural activities.

PEACE CORPS

Another important development reflecting the trend toward a more comprehensive approach was the establishment of the Peace Corps. This program serves to relate a whole new segment of our own human resources to the developmental needs of the underdeveloped countries. Initiated in March, 1961, it was designed to "promote world peace and friendship by making available to interested countries Americans willing to serve overseas who would: 1. Help the people of these countries meet their needs for trained manpower; 2. Help promote a better understanding of the American people on the part of peoples served, and 3. To promote a better understanding of other peoples on the part of the American people."[82]

By the end of the first fiscal year, operating with an initial appropriation of $30 million, the Peace Corps reported 1,051 volunteers serving overseas in 17 countries, and 1,838 additional volunteers in training. The extraordinary appeal of this program, both in the United States and in the countries receiving its services, suggests how deeply felt on both sides is the need for the kind of direct, personal cooperation that the Peace Corps makes possible. In meeting this need with imaginativeness and skill, the program can make a major contribution to the cultural relations of the United States.

THE UNITED NATIONS AND ITS SPECIALIZED AGENCIES

The United Nations and its specialized agencies from their creation in 1945 had been working to develop world-wide cultural cooperation along several different lines: to advance knowledge by fostering the educational, scientific, and artistic resources of mankind; to promote human welfare through a cooperative approach to major world problems of poverty, disease, illiteracy, malnutrition, and world communication; to advance international understanding among the peoples of the world. Their achievements were in many respects modest, in part because of limited funds provided by member states and in part because of the impact of the cold war upon the institutions of international cooperation. Nevertheless, the U.N. agencies made significant progress in promoting important research on such subjects as desalinizing sea water and increasing arability of desert lands; control of epidemics that endanger human and animal health; outer space; and improving agricultural seeds. They have helped to develop world-wide attacks upon illiteracy, disease, and malnutrition; they have achieved reductions in barriers to international trade in educational, scientific, and artistic materials; they have promoted accessibility to people everywhere of more objective knowledge about the history of nations and peoples and the differences among their cultures. A major role has been played by these U.N. agencies in mobilizing technical assistance to be available on a wholly nonpolitical, nonnational basis to the vast underdeveloped areas of the world.

A thoroughly effective relationship between the work of the U.N. agencies and bilateral activities of the United States has not yet been achieved and remains an issue of major importance to the fashioning of the U.S. governmental cultural program.

As the United Nations embarks upon its "Decade of Development" the United States as the principal contributor is faced by the need to appraise with care the advantages and disadvantages of increasing the share of its own educational and technical assistance effort that should be channeled through the multilateral agencies.

Again, in the area of information activities there is great need for strengthening the role of the U.N. and its specialized agencies, and correspondingly adjusting the activities of the United States. In this area the U.N. could play a unique role in establishing direct communication to the peoples of the world community on matters of U.N. policy, program, and action. The absence of channels for such communication is a major barrier to understanding of the U.N. itself, and therefore to the strengthening of the world community. The achievement of the overriding objective of American foreign policy—a genuinely effective United Nations community—requires that the United States further the development of direct information services by the U.N. A challenging opportunity to make available channels for such U.N. services is provided by the development of communication satellites such as Telstar—a medium peculiarly appropriate for use as a channel through which the U.N. could regularly report directly to the people of the world community.

We have seen that over the past 25 years the U.S. government has become progressively involved in a wide variety of cultural activities throughout the world—including such diverse elements as exchanges of students and professional people, information broadcasts, libraries, cultural centers, technical assistance, and overseas presentations in the arts. Most of these activities were initiated under pressure of world events or in direct response to challenges or threats from without: the penetration of Latin America by propaganda from Nazi Germany; the urgent postwar need for reeducation of the occupied countries; the barrage of anti-American propaganda from the U.S.S.R.; the rising demand of the underdeveloped countries for educational and technical help. Other activities represented government efforts to support or supplement programs primarily undertaken by private agencies—for example, the promotion of scholarly interchange or support of American schools abroad. Still others were cooperative ventures with other governments, growing out of our commitments to the U.N. and other international bodies, especially Unesco, WHO, FAO, ILO, the World Bank, the International Atomic Energy Organization, and the Organization of American States.

In the course of these developments many questions of policy arose and were debated, intermittently and with more or less ardor, both within the government and among interested groups in the general public.

One of the most hotly debated issues, as we have seen, was that of the proper balance between short-term, "maximum impact" activities of a propaganda character and the longer-term programs such as educational exchanges, joint scientific and cultural undertakings, and technical assistance. In time of war or great international tension the former tended to dominate the scene. Relaxation of tension brought a swing of the pendulum toward greater emphasis on the long-range measures.

Another persistent question concerned the proper relationship between governmental and private agencies in the various types of cultural activity involved. Should the role of government be limited generally to stimulating, encouraging, assisting, and supplementing private effort? Or should the government actively initiate programs required by the exigencies of foreign policy, enlist the cooperation of the private sector, and direct the activities undertaken?

What administrative pattern, both in Washington and in the field, can best facilitate the government's performance of its role? Should all cultural activities be directed by one agency, or should they be dispersed among various agencies, and if the latter, how can they be effectively coordinated? And how should the administration of cultural activities be coordinated with that of related activities such as economic development assistance or trade?

To what extent should the transnational cultural programs of the United States be deliberately related to those of other countries, and should this be done primarily through multilateral means or through bilateral, reciprocal means? For that matter, to what extent *can* cultural relations be made genuinely reciprocal?

What should be the magnitude of an adequate total cultural relations program, and what should be the relative magnitude of each of its component parts?

These questions, and many others like them, have been the subjects of discussion in innumerable studies, reports, conference sessions, Congressional hearings, etc., as a conscious search for over-all policy has developed and become increasingly insistent.[83]

Underlying all these questions, and in a sense conditioning the answers to all of them, are the fundamental questions: *What are the overriding objectives of United States foreign policy? Can cultural programs contribute to their advancement? If so, how?*

The quarter-century during which the United States has been experimenting with cultural relations programs has been a period of momentous changes in the world setting for which foreign policies are designed. As new policy objectives have evolved to meet the demands of a dramatically changed world, the potential significance of cultural activities as means toward these objectives has come sharply into focus. At the same time, experience with a wide range of activities, however haphazard and sporadic, has given valuable insight into the unique character of their contribution.

It is the question of relevance to basic objectives, therefore, that will concern us primarily as we turn, in the remainder of this book, to the future role of cultural activities in U.S. foreign policy. We shall need to examine, in broad outline, (1) the probable world setting in which the international relations of the United States will be conducted, (2) the major foreign policies required for such a setting, (3) the contribution that cultural relations activities can make to the success of those policies, and (4) the requirements for an effective cultural relations program.

PART II

The Role
of Cultural Activities

FIVE

The World Setting

THE CUMULATIVE result of 25 years of experimentation with
various kinds of cultural programs has been the emergence of cultural
activities as a major factor in conduct of the United States foreign relations. The implications of this development have not, however,
been sufficiently thought through by the executive branch, by the
Congress, or by the American people.

The importance of this dimension derives both from the nature
of U.S. foreign policy objectives and from the specific kind of contribution that cultural relations can make to the attainment of these
objectives.

The United States finds itself, in the early nineteen-sixties, bur-
dened with responsibilities of leadership in a world of unparalleled
complexity and danger: a world in which the fate of every country is deeply interrelated with that of every other, and in which the
possibility of genuinely independent action by any nation has almost
totally disappeared.

While the number of sovereign states has vastly increased and independent national identity is everywhere fiercely asserted and defended, sovereignty becomes more and more meaningless with each
scientific and technological advance. Satellites, man-made and controlled, orbit the earth, making a mockery of national boundaries.
Intercontinental missiles threaten nuclear destruction in any part of
the globe. Communications have obliterated distance, bringing us

face to face with the most remote peoples and compelling us to reckon with their problems as well as our own.

The economic life of every industrialized nation is deeply intertwined with that of many others. The progress of advanced national economies is contingent upon access to raw materials held by other countries; no nation is industrially self-sufficient. The widening variety of the products of industry and agriculture demands an outlet in a larger volume of international trade. The continuing expansion of large-scale production, accelerated by automation, likewise requires world-wide markets. Even the least industrialized country may find its economy suddenly ruined by a drop in the world price of a key agricultural product. The intricate, shifting patterns of international investment, finance, and trade intimately affect the domestic economies of all countries, advanced or underdeveloped.

In such an interrelated world, each nation is faced with an ever-growing agenda of problems, world-wide in scope, that defy solution on a national basis—problems that demand planned and coordinated action by many countries. These problems range all the way from such routine matters as the regulation of air traffic, the control of epidemics, the facilitation of exports and imports, or the prediction and control of the weather, to the overshadowing problem of how to prevent mutual annihilation by nuclear war. Almost every so-called "domestic" problem has its international aspect; the sharp line between internal and external affairs has become hopelessly blurred.

As problems requiring international solutions arose and became increasingly acute during the past half century, a large variety of cooperative arrangements was gradually developed to cope with them jointly, and the outlines of a world-wide community began to be reflected in comprehensive world-wide organizations—first in the League of Nations, and then in the United Nations after the second World War had demonstrated overwhelmingly the global nature of the issues that most deeply affected the well-being of individual countries.

In the United Nations Charter a long step was taken toward defining the objectives of the emerging world community, and creating mechanisms to achieve these objectives. The assumptions underlying the Charter are essentially those evolved by the Western democratic countries in the course of their national development:

that diversity is good, and essential; that the individual has the right to develop his own potential capacities to the fullest extent consistent with the equal rights of others; that conflicting interests and desires can be adjusted peaceably through processes of law; that common goals can be identified, and that mechanisms can be devised through which voluntary efforts can be concerted for their achievement.

These assumptions, applied to nations as well as to individuals, underlie the constitutions of the United Nations, the specialized agencies, and many of the international instruments of the free world with more limited tasks and more limited membership. They were presumably accepted, tacitly if not explicitly, by all the nations that became members of the United Nations organization. To most of the Western nations, at least, they seem to be an indispensable minimum upon which a genuine world community can be based.

It is not unreasonable to suppose that if these assumptions had been wholeheartedly acted upon by all signatories of the Charter, the U.N. system established in 1945 could have evolved gradually but steadily into a world community capable of maintaining peace and developing orderly processes for dealing with the world's common business.

The fortunes of the U.N. during the past seventeen years have made vividly clear, however, that these basic assumptions are not accepted by all its members. From the beginning there have existed side by side within the organization two major competing concepts of world community (not including the Fascist view held by a few governments). These two concepts reflect conflicting views of human rights, of social organization, of history itself.

According to the Marxist ideology professed by the Communist members of the U.N., the true world community is one which must come about not by mutual accommodation and adjustment among diverse national states, but by the ultimate inevitable triumph of Communism over "capitalism," on a world-wide scale. Negotiation, compromise, cooperation within the framework of international organizations or otherwise, on the basis of a body of mutually accepted principles such as those in the U.N. Charter—all these are regarded by Communist dogma merely as tactical tools to be used when they can serve to sharpen class conflict and thus hasten the ultimate overturn of the social order, out of which can then arise the Marxist world order of Communism. Thus it is not illogical from the Communist point of view to use these tools alternately, or even simultaneously, with such other tools as subversion, deception, domination, and violence.

Surely it is one of the great ironies of history that the slow evolution of a democratically-based cooperative world order reached the stage of organization into genuinely global institutions at the time (1945) when the proponents of a Communist world order had succeeded in establishing firm control within several of the world's national states, thus acquiring power to use the organs of the newly created United Nations for their own purposes.

If the Communist states were committed by their own basic philosophy to play a divisive and disruptive role within the United Nations, the non-Communist members were no less committed by their concept of universal world order to keep the Communist members in the U.N. system; to counter their subversive moves within the U.N. and within other member states only by measures consistent with the Charter; to make whatever progress was possible toward an effective world community, despite the obstructive tactics of Communist members; and to hope for a gradual expansion of the areas in which self-interest or even some modification in their objectives might induce at least their partial cooperation rather than recalcitrance.

The cold war of the 1950s and 1960s has often been depicted as simply a power struggle between the United States and the U.S.S.R. or between the free nations and the Communist nations, with territorial expansion of the Communist empire a primary challenge, and "containment" the principal response. A more comprehensive view is that which sees the cold war as a conflict between two contrasting concepts of world order. In such a conflict victory may depend not so much on armed might as on the firmness of each side's commitment to its own principles. Basically it is a conflict of ideas, between the Communist concept of a world community based on totalitarian principles and the democratic concept of a world community based on diversity, with unity voluntarily achieved and maintained through freely accepted commitments to democratically evolved "rules of the game." The test of strength is as much a test of conviction, commitment, and consistency of action as it is of military power. The

Communist concept of world order is aggressive, class-based, theoretically monolithic; the U.N. concept is democratic, cooperative, pluralistic. The Communist concept is based on the conviction that the ultimate triumph of Communism is inevitable—that an inexorable destiny is on the side of its champions. The U.N. concept is of a world community that is not inevitable but must be fought for—that can be achieved by sustained effort, mutual persuasion, joint exploration of problems, mutual assistance on tasks of recognized common concern, and voluntary self-discipline in the general interest.

The crucial cold war question for the non-Communist nations is not, therefore, merely whether they can maintain military superiority and prevent the expansion of the Communist empire, but whether they can, as free peoples, pull themselves together into a genuine world community of sufficient inner strength and dynamism to meet the challenge, whatever its form, and to proceed steadily with the constructive business of world development—including the ultimate involvement of the Communists in this process, despite the apparently irreconcilable nature of their world philosophy.

There is increasing evidence that this effective involvement may not be as remote a possibility as it has seemed in the past. Although the Marxian theory professed by the Communist countries appears to provide a unifying ideology for each of them individually and for the Communist countries collectively, the reality of politics both within and among these nations is quite different. The historical origins of Marxism gave it a theoretical framework that has proved difficult to apply to the actual industrial world of the twentieth century. This has led to disputes over its meaning and utility among rival individuals and factions, both within and among the Communist countries. The political power structure of Communism may be totalitarian, but it is far from monolithic on either the national or the world scene. The degrees of internal difference and articulate protest of course vary from country to country, but there is clear evidence that neither the pure Marxian theory nor the particular interpretations of it by governments now in power are unquestioningly accepted by the entire population of any Communist country. The world-wide differences among national Communist parties or governments is great, as is shown in competing claims to orthodoxy and the popularity of many varieties of "Titoism."

In short, neither pure nineteenth-century Marxian ideology nor the particular interpretations of it espoused by individual Communist persons, parties, or countries should be assumed to be lasting or unchanging. The viability of the United Nations system and its capacity to accommodate the Communist countries within the diversity of its total membership may be one of the factors determining the direction of Communist political evolution. It may also influence the readiness of Communist governments to honor their United Nations obligations.

Among the industrialized, democratically-oriented Western nations, the effort to develop close political, military, and economic cooperation has begun to show dramatic results, despite the intricate and baffling problems encountered at every turn. Within the U.N., in spite of great difficulties, there is growing evidence of a pulling together by member states really committed to the U.N. concept, and of their determination to make it work. NATO, for all its ups and downs, remains a powerful bulwark against overt aggression. The European Economic Community, after years of experimenting, has achieved an impressive degree of integration in the economic life of its member states, and has moved on, ahead of schedule, to the second stage of development. The thorny problem of how to achieve the participation of Great Britain and other European nations in the economic community is the subject of sustained and determined efforts. The harmonious relating of the United States and British Commonwealth economies to this central core of cooperation is in process of active negotiation. Very grave problems still remain to be solved, but the disastrous effects of economic warfare among the leaders of the free world are acutely recognized, and the rapidly rising industrial power of the Communist bloc exerts added pressure for progress toward integration. The so-called "de Gaulle crisis" early in 1963 was a serious set-back, but the forces making for unity are still strong, and must prevail if Europe and the West are to survive.

Political cooperation among the industrialized free world nations, both within the U.N. and outside it, has been hampered by conflicting views on colonial policy, by divergent concepts of military strategy, by retrogressive concepts of sovereignty, by ancient jealousies and rivalries that often refuse to be wholly subdued even in the face of common danger. Here, again, progress is slow—but there appear to be grounds for optimism in the more intensive recent efforts toward improved communication and greater consultation among the Western allies over the whole range of political problems. Gradually the early postwar situation, in which the United States dominated because of its military and economic power, is being replaced by one in which the other Western countries increasingly challenge any effort of the United States unilaterally to determine the course of world affairs. Slowly but with increasing effectiveness the Western nations, including the United States, are learning to engage in joint planning, joint policy development, and joint administration in areas of joint concern.

The task of building and maintaining an effective free world community despite the disruptive efforts of the Communist countries would be difficult enough if it involved merely the forging of a common will and the charting of common courses of action among the Western, industrialized, democratic members of the U.N. community. It is made infinitely more difficult by the sudden emergence on the world scene of a large group of newly independent nations, mostly in Asia and Africa, which, as full-fledged members of the U.N., are presumably committed to the concepts of a free world community embodied in the Charter, but which are, for the most part, unwilling to identify themselves with either side in the continuing struggle to put these concepts into effective operation.

The fierce preoccupation of these countries with maintaining their national independence might be expected to align them automatically with the non-Communist countries, which welcome diversity and cooperation among nations. The logic of this is sometimes obscured for them, however, by the fact that the leaders of the free world community include their former colonial masters, most vividly associated in their minds with oppression or at least denial of their freedom. Moreover, the ideological conflict as such often has relatively little meaning for them. With limited experience in the actual workings of either democracy or Communism, they sometimes see little to choose between the rival ideologies, which use many of the same words—"democracy," "equality," "peace," "progress," "cooperation"—though with totally different meanings. With few exceptions, however, they have not shown any intention to tie their future to the Communist world. Certainly they remain uncommitted on the specious issue of capitalism versus socialism, which the Communists have tried to identify as the issue of greatest concern for the under-developed countries. They are often less concerned with the phi-losophies and ideologies underlying the world community—or even those underlying their own political systems—than with the pressing demands of their burgeoning populations: demands for a higher standard of living, for education, for improved health and nutrition, for land reform, for industrialization. The extent of their political experience and development has not led them to refine their con-ceptions of the nature of politics, the role of government and of the citizen. They have had little occasion to appraise the substantive im-portance of U.N. concepts for the success of their own development.

These primary concerns are shared by another large group of coun-tries, mostly in Latin America, who have a longer history of political independence but whose economic and social development has not kept pace with the times.

Most of the pressing objectives of the underdeveloped countries can be attained only with assistance from the more economically ad-vanced countries. That they should get this assistance without loss or impairment of their freedom of action as independent nations is of vital importance to the free world, because they are an indispensable component of any conceivable world order based upon free, voluntary cooperation. The underdeveloped countries, taken together, represent the larger part of the world's population—and that proportion is in-creasing rapidly. Their membership in the United Nations has shifted the balance of power in the Assembly so that, voting together, they can exert a determining influence upon its action. Their human and natural resources, once developed, can contribute immeasura-bly to the strength of the free world community; even at a semi-industrialized stage, they contribute much to the economic life of the world. On the other hand, their absorption willingly or by force into the totalitarian empires could profoundly affect the free world's chances of survival.

Among the most fateful questions of our time, therefore, are those concerning the newly developing countries of the world. Can these countries, already linked to the free world community through membership in the United Nations, successfully complete the eco-nomic, social, and political revolutions now sweeping them and

come out equipped with the necessary requirements for full participation in such a community? If they are to become fully effective
partners in the free world, they must achieve and maintain genuine
national independence, with whatever freedom of choice remains to
any modern nation. They must achieve viable nationhood; governments responsive to the will of the people, even though the latter
may not yet be prepared for democratic institutions; dynamic economies; sufficient education to make democratic institutions as well as
economic development increasingly feasible; recognition by their national leaders of the stake the developing nation has in a free world
order; and willingness to play a constructive role in its evolution.

The shape of the future world will depend very much upon the
degree to which the national policies of the economically advanced
free countries can speed these processes and make whatever adjustments are necessary to integrate the new nations harmoniously into
the existing patterns of the world community.

In this world setting the interests of the United States will best be
served by policies that contribute most directly to the further development of a world community of those nations that wish to abide
by the principles of the United Nations. We must seek to bring into
more effective relationship with this community those nations which,
for whatever reasons, have been reluctant so far to accept in reality
the obligations of the U.N. Charter. In pursuing this objective, we
must be ready to accept diversity and pluralism of social systems
within this community so long as these do not deny the principles
and beliefs upon which the United Nations rests.

The task we face in pursuing this foreign policy objective is of a
magnitude that can hardly be overstated. It will not be completed
within this century. It demands constant attention to the problem of
welding together into some kind of working unity what is still a
heterogeneous congeries of sovereign peoples (including ourselves),
different in traditions and values, unequal in wealth and power, many
inexperienced in democratic procedures, preoccupied with their own
troubles, impatient, quarrelsome, and often irresponsibly independent. It demands a continuing effort toward identification of common
goals, the building of mutual confidence, the devising of joint
plans of action. It demands, above all, the generation of a common
will strong enough to make of the free world community a living,

dynamic force rather than a logical abstraction. It demands a continuing search for ways of weakening the appeal of Communism and of disproving its alleged monolithic character.

Among the means available for promoting the achievement of free world unity, the United Nations still remains the most important single instrumentality, if only because it represents the sole existing political framework for the world-wide community of all nations which is the ultimate goal.

The experience of its stormy first years has shown how deep are the cleavages that divide its members and how remote are the prospects for resolving all their differences. It has made clear, too, as we have seen, the basic rejection by most of its Communist members of the very purposes for which the U.N. exists, and their deliberate use of its mechanisms for preventing agreement and effective action.

Certainly we must not expect quick results from the United Nations. But neither should we allow the heartbreaking slowness of its processes to deter us from steadfast commitment to it and participation in it. Viewed in the perspective of history, it is something of a miracle that an institution as revolutionary in concept and purpose as the United Nations should have survived at all in the continuing crises of the postwar years. Its growth in strength and effectiveness, however slow, represents the growing capacity of the world as a whole, with all its conflicting interests, to put into the actual practice of international relations the principles upon which our own and other democratic societies are founded. The more nearly universal is its membership, the slower but also the more significant is its growth. In its ultimate maturing lies our best hope of a peaceful and orderly world, congenial to our preferred way of life. United States policy, then, must take realistically into account both the potential significance of the United Nations and its present inadequacy, and must seek both to strengthen and to supplement it in the actual conduct of our foreign relations.

This means that the long-range, over-all objective of building a genuine free world community has to be pursued not only within the U.N. framework but also in all the infinitely complex, day-to-day relationships with individual countries and groups of countries. The ways by which we pursue the basic objective will obviously differ in relations with different countries and groups of countries, depending upon the degree of their commitment to the U.N. principles, their experience as independent nations, and their traditional and current attitudes toward cooperation with the United States. While the immediate context for United States foreign policies varies in each individual nation, three major groups can be identified for the purpose of defining policies that will carry us toward our long-range objective.

In our relations with those countries in Europe, the Americas, Asia, and the British Commonwealth that are committed to U.N. principles through long traditions and experience, foreign policy should be guided by the objective of finding ever greater common ground and more effective joint approaches to the urgent economic, political, and social problems that we share with them. United States initiative is needed in reconciling our conflicting trade interests and working out means for economic cooperation; in concerting efforts to aid the developing countries; in maintaining unity of purpose and action vis-à-vis the Communist nations; in promoting common and mutually acceptable approaches to issues in the United Nations.

These are the nations that we must count upon as our most reliable partners in the joint venture of building a free world community. Unless we can achieve unity of purpose and effectiveness of cooperation with them, there is little hope for success in the broader task.

This is not by any means simply a matter of persuading other Western countries to pursue enlightened policies of international cooperation. Adjustments in our own policies may be far more crucial, since during the postwar years we have tended to have our own way in relations with the West. Our military superiority and our economic power, combined with the military and economic exhaustion of western Europe, gave us in effect a controlling voice in programs for Western economic recovery and military defense. Today the vigor of western European economies is obvious, as is also their ability to support a larger proportion of the joint Western defense burden and the costs of assisting newly developing countries. The political consequences are manifest in a new, truly revolutionary spirit among western European countries in fashioning new kinds of economic and political communities. But the political consequence is also seen in their determination to participate effectively in the many kinds of political, economic, and military decision-making which had often been left to us, even though the forms of shared responsibility were observed.

Europe's new-found freedom of action, based on economic recovery combined with successful evolution toward political integration, faces the United States with another historic opportunity to speed the achievement of a world community. It is comparable to the opportunities we seized in helping to establish the United Nations, in launching the Marshall Plan, and in developing the Point Four program.

The opportunity is to assist in the development of new ways of planning jointly with the western European countries our foreign policy objectives and the means for attaining them. This will undoubtedly mean the strengthening of institutions for the joint management of our defense (North Atlantic Treaty Organization) and of our economic relationships (Organization for Economic Cooperation and Development), as well as for more effective political collaboration (Atlantic Council). But whatever the developments in this area, they must be consistent with and give support to the major objective of a strong world community of the United Nations. The direction in the growth and evolution of these Western cooperative arrangements should generally be toward greater universality of participation and therefore toward ultimate identification with the U.N. community in scope and in membership.

Japan occupies a unique place in the foreign relations of the United States. It cannot be classified as Western, Communist, or underdeveloped. Historically and racially it sometimes seems similar to the economically underdeveloped countries, but scientifically, technologically, and industrially it ranks with the most developed countries of the West. Defeated by the West in the last war and subjected to occupation rule until 1950, its alignment with the West today depends upon the willingness of the West to encourage Japanese economic growth through the negotiation of rational trade arrangements and its participation in the joint planning of international policies. Meanwhile, its political and economic power are the objects of covetous Communist ambitions ,while its technical assistance and capital are needed especially by southeast Asian countries only recently recovered from the war-time ravages of the Japanese military.

Our primary objective in respect to Japan must clearly be its continuous alignment with the West, both to resist Communist pressures and to assist in the underdeveloped countries. Japan's participation in the building of a strong world community is essential for the United States and all the Western countries.

In relation to the U.S.S.R., Communist China, and their satellites, we must obviously maintain, together with our allies, sufficient military strength to deter them from actual attack upon us, and we must continue to oppose their aggressive expansion at the expense of other countries, whether this expansion is attempted by overt military action or by subversion or economic domination. At the same time we must make every effort to resolve our conflicts with them by peaceful means, through the U.N. if possible, outside it if necessary.

The obvious lack of unity among the several Communist countries opens immense opportunities for diplomatic action designed to make more attractive to each of them a genuinely constructive role in the United Nations community. We must be aware that powerful and authoritarian as their governments may be, the Communist systems have not attained their proclaimed goals at home, and that their people do not represent a solid unthinking mass, indifferent to or unaware of the shortcomings of Communism in theory and in practice. There are cleavages, doubts, conflicts, uncertainties, and other signs of real and potential disaffection that belie the alleged monolithic image long held before us. We must make every effort to get through to the peoples of countries dominated by Communism, in the hope of extending the range of normal human relationships with them. Such contacts may serve to lessen tensions, counteract the false image of the West projected by their government propaganda, implant the concepts of a cooperative world order, and keep before them as a live reality the democratic alternative to Communism. Not only must a firm military shield be visible to those Communist leaders who contemplate aggression, but a prospect for participation in the world community must be clear to persons within the Communist countries who would prefer this goal in their own foreign policies.

In our policies toward the newly developing countries of Africa, Asia, the Middle East, and Latin America, we must be guided by recognition of the fact that by sheer weight of numbers, population, and geographic extent they represent a crucially important element in any potential world community. Most of them are already members of the U.N. and are thus committed in theory at least to the kind of free world association that is consistent with our interests. Despite the concerted drive of the Communist governments to win their favor, only a few have committed themselves to Communist ideology or to alliance with the Soviet Union or Communist China.

But most of them are still relatively unprepared for participating as full partners in a world community that is based upon voluntary cooperation among self-reliant, responsible sovereign states. We must, of course, help them to resist encroachments upon their territory and exploitation of their weaknesses by any powers that would establish domination over them. But this kind of help is futile unless comple-mented by assistance in modernizing their economies, raising the standards of living and improving the health and nutrition of their peoples, building social and political institutions, establishing a broad base of educated citizens, and developing quickly the technically trained manpower they so desperately need. Our own self-interest re-quires that we give them as much help as we possibly can in attaining all these critical objectives, and that we give our assistance in a way that demonstrates the genuineness of our own commitment to the principles on which the free world community is founded. By our trade policies, by our policies in the U.N., by our day-to-day political and diplomatic relationships, and, above all, by the cooperative in-volvement of the American people in joint efforts toward meeting their urgent needs, we can deliberately facilitate their progressive integration into the free world community and help them stand on their own feet as self-respecting, creative, responsible participants in its growth.

Pursuit of the policy objectives described above through the day-to-day conduct of U. S. foreign relations calls for the use of all the varied resources available to the national government. Political-diplo-matic resources, reinforced by the military, are the ones traditionally relied upon most heavily. Since the first World War, the resources of economic policy have come to play an enormously important part. The still more recent addition of cultural resources, described in the historical chapters of this book, has provided a third dimension to United States foreign policy: a dimension that serves to give depth, stability, and a forward-looking orientation to the relations between the United States and the other members of the evolving world community.

The nature of the contribution that cultural action can make to the achievement of our foreign policy objectives will be discussed in the following chapter.

SIX

Cultural Relations and Foreign Policy Objectives

CULTURAL RELATIONS have only recently become a part of the conduct of U.S. foreign relations, as the historical review has made clear. They constitute a dimension that has been added under pressure of world events and as an outgrowth of the increasing interdependence among the sovereign states of the world community. They include educational, scientific, and broadly humanistic exchanges, technical assistance of many kinds, and information activities. They involve the transnational communication of knowledge, skills, ideas, and values.

What contribution can cultural activities make to the achievement of the basic U.S. foreign policy objectives outlined above? This can best be seen in the separate contexts of our relations with the Western, the Communist, and the less developed countries. In using this three-way grouping of nations, it must be emphasized that there is great variety among the countries in each group and in our relations with them. Relations with Germany, France, Italy, and the United Kingdom all differ in detail and in specific day-to-day issues. The same is true of U.S. relations with Yugoslavia, Poland, Czechoslovakia, and the U.S.S.R. Variety is great also in our relationships with countries such as Lebanon, Indonesia, Nigeria, Egypt, India, and

156

Peru. But there are enough similarities in our relations with all members of each of the three groups to make this classification a convenient device for examining the contribution that cultural activities can make to the conduct of U.S. foreign relations.

WESTERN COUNTRIES

It is clear that we must rely primarily upon cooperation with the other Western countries for the achievement of all our objectives. They share with us the values and concepts fundamental to a dynamic, cohesive, and effective free world society; their resources are indispensable in the effort to resist Communist aggression and promote the modernization of the underdeveloped countries. Together, we constitute a partnership that is the nucleus of the growing world community.

The strength and vitality of this partnership depend in part upon the continuing growth of the educational, scientific, technological, and artistic resources of the Western community itself. Progress in the development of these resources was responsible for the role of world leadership enjoyed by the West during the last two centuries. But vital political, technological, and social changes now taking place throughout the world present new challenges that can be met by the West only by further growth in their combined scientific, educational, and technological resources.

At the same time, the leadership of the Western community of nations depends upon mutual understanding and upon continued conviction among us that we are guided by common purposes, common values, and mutual respect.

Exchanges of knowledge, skills, ideas, and values are fundamental both to the further development of Western resources and to the strengthening of understanding among us. The adequacy of such exchanges must therefore be of vital concern to the U.S. government.

There is much in the relationships between the United States and the other Western countries that makes for easy cooperation. A common historical tradition going back to Greco-Roman times has produced important similarities in values, in philosophy and intellectual development, in institutions of government, in methods of commerce, and in social organization. During our own colonial period (as in those of Canada, Australia, and New Zealand) this background was transplanted by immigrant settlers, and the process was continued throughout the nineteenth century and well into the twentieth. Our immigrant stock has always been of predominantly Western origin (English, Irish, Scotch, Scandinavian, German, Italian, Polish).

This common background has given rise to a vast network of communication in every important field. Much of this comes in day-to-day negotiations on matters of international trade and investment, patents, and so on, plus the contacts generated by business organizations. Professional people—doctors, engineers, lawyers, scholars, city planners, architects, writers, artists, agriculturalists, educators—on both sides of the Atlantic keep in touch with one another individually and through various professional associations, comparing and sharing knowledge and skills, and working both cooperatively and competitively on problems of common concern. Religious agencies, universities, and the mass media are all deeply involved in the intricate network of communication among Western countries. Private foundations, both American and foreign, make grants to scholars, students, and institutions to encourage the advancement of education, science, technology, and the arts on the basis of transnational cooperation. Western educational systems, though different in many respects, have important features in common and aspire to similar standards of quality and professional competence. This myriad of cultural relationships is reinforced by family ties and extensive tourism.

The common heritage and the experience of mutual advancement resulting from a wide spectrum of essentially private cultural exchanges have provided sufficient mutual comprehension to make possible relatively harmonious relations between the United States and Western-oriented countries, and agreement upon certain standards of conduct basic to the United Nations system.

But there are also factors that militate against the further development of Western cooperation. Among these are all the normal competitive aspects of our Western relationships, such as trade, which can become divisive influences unless they are expressed in terms of mutual benefit to be derived from competition. The postwar disparity in productivity, in economic and military power, in size, and in wealth between the United States and other countries of the West has frequently given rise to jealousy and distrust on the part of the latter. On the other hand, the past decade has seen a great upward surge in the economies of most of the European countries, particularly those of the Common Market, and there is increasing evidence that alarm over the slower growth rate in the United States and increasing competition from Europe may lead to a similar feeling of hostility in this country. Historical differences on colonialism and other issues have cut deeply into the fabric of understanding and still seriously damage the prospect for effective cooperation. Communist propaganda seeks deliberately to exploit all these differences among the Western countries.

These discordant elements have been manifested in the course of many political crises. There has been frequent Western discord on the role, authority, and command structure of NATO, revealing lack of understanding of the implications of a joint defense structure. More recently there has been acute conflict over the proposal for a European nuclear force. In the Suez crisis France, the United Kingdom, and Israel found the United States opposed to their action, which we saw as a flagrant violation of United Nations obligations. Colonial and postcolonial policies in Asia and Africa have led to great strains among the Western countries. The finding of a common Western response to the chronic Berlin crisis has at times seemed as difficult as resolving the issue with the Soviet Union.

The divisive factors that endanger Western solidarity can be considerably mitigated by the continued expansion of those normal cultural exchanges that have in the past provided the foundations for Western unity. The contribution that government can make toward this end is first of all to encourage further development of the network of private cultural communications with other Western countries. This is the basic reason for having in Washington and at the embassies in Europe a governmental staff concerned with educational and cultural affairs. But this is clearly not enough, in view of the urgent need for closer cooperation with the West. The role of the government should be not merely to facilitate private efforts, but whenever necessary to supplement them by carrying on specific activities in which private agencies may not be interested, for which they may lack adequate resources, or which they may not be qualified to undertake.

Such a positive role for government should include continuing for the indefinite future educational exchange programs of the type financed under the Fulbright-Hays Act: exchanges of scholars, teachers, lecturers, students, specialists, and leaders in many fields. The amount of public financing provided for this purpose must be based on a continuing appraisal of needs, country by country, and on a clear policy decision to involve in these experiences as many qualified people as possible.

Our government should also continue to support the development of American studies in schools and universities of Western countries in order to provide increasing knowledge and understanding of the United States among their peoples. The trend toward closer economic and political integration among the Western nations, including the United States, clearly demands that a stronger base of mutual understanding be provided by the educational institutions in each country. Until this is adequately provided by other governments or by private resources, the U.S. government must continue to concern itself with this problem. The establishment of international universities such as that planned by the Council of Europe at Florence, and of international research institutes, will clearly be needed and will require a high degree of initiative and assistance from government.

Essential cultural activities that private agencies are not equipped to undertake include cultural and information centers designed to provide a "window to America." Private agencies cannot be expected to maintain such centers, which entail substantial costs justified only in the broad public interest, and which depend for their libraries, displays, exhibits, lectures, musical programs, and information services upon coordinated support from several government agencies as well as from many private sources. Their long-term cumulative impact depends upon long-term budgetary commitments. These centers are for hundreds of thousands of persons almost the sole opportunity to improve their knowledge of American life and culture. The libraries alone, with their wide selection of American books and their easy accessibility through open shelves, are revealing symbols and interpreters of life in the United States.

Mass media are among the most important forces making for mutual understanding—or misunderstanding—among Western peoples.

Privately owned media are motivated by commercial profit, which inevitably limits the volume, scope, and treatment of their news and feature coverage. Only the government can afford, for reasons of national interest, the costs of certain types of mass media programs undertaken deliberately to increase understanding and a greater sense of unity among the Western nations.

The government should therefore continue its special feature news stories, its magazine and pamphlet publications, and the quick wire transmission of news about current U.S. developments, including full texts of speeches by the President or Secretary of State. It should also continue its successful radio activities in the form of recordings suitable for rebroadcast by foreign stations and television news and feature programs. Filmed information programs are still important for exhibition in commercial theaters and on television. The government undoubtedly must continue its central role in assuring world-wide all-media coverage for major events such as the American space flights. It should also play a central role in assuring linkage of U.S. television with British, French, Italian, and West German facilities through Eurovision.

Government alone can provide support for the many intergovernmental institutions that engage in cultural activities. Foremost among these are the specialized agencies of the United Nations: Unesco, WHO, FAO, ILO, AEO, and others. Created largely through the initiative of Western countries, they represent a major attempt to provide international instrumentalities for projecting into the larger world community the methods of collaboration found successful within and among individual Western countries. They provide cooperative world-wide resources for the Western countries to draw upon in their common task of assisting newly developing countries. They provide, also, an important institutional framework through which to involve the Communist countries and their people in the work of the world community. It is clearly in the interest of the United States to strengthen the U.N. agencies by every possible means and to utilize them whenever this is feasible.

United States participation with other Western countries in strengthening these global agencies is not inconsistent with the development of exclusively Western cooperative institutions. An especially important Western regional agency that encourages cultural relations among its member states is the Organization for Economic Cooperation and Development, successor to the Organization of European Economic Cooperation. The OECD, of which the United States is a member, promotes policies designed "to achieve the highest sustainable economic growth . . . and a rising standard of living in member countries. . . ; to contribute to sound economic expansion in member as well as non-member countries . . . ; and . . . to the expansion of world trade. . . ."[1]

One of the OECD's major objectives is to strengthen the intellectual resources of the member countries. For example, its member states are now engaged in appraising their educational systems. This appraisal is designed to lay the groundwork for educational cooperation among Western countries for their mutual benefit and for worldwide economic development. The further development of the OECD along these lines will contribute to closer cooperation among Western countries, will reinforce economic and military cooperation, will enhance their unity for dealing with Communist pressures, and will assist them in responding to the needs of newly developing areas—all important aspects of U.S. foreign policy.

Japan, although geographically far from western Europe and North America, has forced itself through a developmental process that was Western in character and has achieved a stage in education, science, and technology that is comparable to that of most of the Western prototypes. It is part of the Western community in these respects and is committed to foreign policies consistent with the Western concepts of world community.

Among the most critical problems in our relations with Japan are those of a cultural nature. In respect to the language barrier a massive effort is required, promoted by both governments, to increase knowledge of Japanese by Americans and of English by Japanese. Paralleling it is the need of educational and artistic exchanges to promote better mutual understanding, in order to reinforce the cooperation of our governments in the world community. Most kinds of cultural relations, with the exception of technical assistance, are of vital importance for the attainment of our foreign policy objectives in Japan.

COMMUNIST COUNTRIES

In relations with the Communist countries cultural activities play a role of unique importance, since they are almost the only practicable means of penetrating the Iron Curtain. The more we can do this, the more we can learn about Soviet strengths and weaknesses, and the better chance we have of introducing realistic and moderating currents into Soviet thinking and Soviet policies.

The enforced isolation of the Communist peoples from the rest of the world has interrupted the growth of those normal relations between peoples that constitute the supporting framework necessary for peaceful intergovernmental relations. Before the Communists took over there was a substantial history of cultural contacts—resulting from migration, commerce, scholarship, and the arts—between the people of the United States and those of Russia, China, Poland, Czechoslovakia, Rumania, Bulgaria, Hungary, and Yugoslavia. Were it not for the artificial barriers imposed by Communist governments, such contacts would still be taking place. Their absence has undoubtedly helped greatly to exacerbate the tensions of the cold war.

Recently a few chinks have begun to appear in the Iron if not in the Bamboo Curtain. We should spare no effort to take advantage of these in order to introduce into the minds of the peoples under Communist rule, and of their leaders, more accurate ideas than they now have of the actual state of affairs in the outside world. The cultivation of common cultural interests is the most effective means to this end.

THE SOVIET UNION

As we have already seen, the death of Stalin led to some relaxation of the Soviet Union's policy of extreme intellectual isolationism. In 1956 Khrushchev stated: "We must study the capitalist economy attentively . . . study the best that the capitalist countries have to offer . . . and exploit everything in foreign experience that is of use."[2] Khrushchev was especially anxious for access to the technological achievements of the United States. The Russians wanted to get American technical and scientific data while avoiding, so far as possible, the risks of exposure to subversive democratic ideas. The new policy sought also to bring about a change in the Western countries' image of the Soviet system, in order to weaken the resistance of their peoples to Communist pressure. It therefore encouraged the spread of information about Soviet science and technology, and of its theater, ballet, music, and other arts. In return some products of American culture were allowed to enter the Soviet Union. The Soviet government was prepared, on a generally reciprocal basis, to permit access by Americans to Soviet scholarship.

These exchanges were, of course, closely controlled by the Soviet government, which sought to secure maximum benefits to the U.S.S.R. with a minimum of effects that might weaken its people's loyalty. This was the spirit in which the U.S.S.R. undertook to negotiate with the United States the cultural agreements of 1958, 1959, and 1962.

The willingness of the Soviet leaders to increase contacts with the United States was paralleled by signs that the Soviet people were demanding greater access to the cultural products of the West—a mood which has rapidly blossomed in the years since the first official cultural exchange agreement was signed.

It is obviously in the interest of the United States to exploit in every possible way the opportunity that the present situation affords us for establishing closer contacts with the peoples of the U.S.S.R. This is a means to inform ourselves better about the Soviet people, their society and institutions, and the working of their political system. There have been great gaps in our knowledge—gaps of importance to scholars, to the American people as a whole, and to the U.S. government—which can now be narrowed.

Moreover, the cultural communications now permitted allow us to counteract, if only in a small way, the distorted image of the United States which the Soviet government seeks to convey to its people. Visitors from the United States—tourists, scholars, musicians, scientists, technicians, the personnel of trade fairs and other exhibitions—can give to Soviet citizens some first-hand impressions that must contribute to a more critical and informed appraisal of the official propaganda about the United States issued by the Soviet government. The visits to the United States of Soviet citizens in any exchange capacity afford them not only opportunities to bring to Americans a corresponding first-hand impression of what individual Russians are like; they also enable Soviet citizens to observe American society and to communicate what they learn to others upon their return home. Finally, the cultural exchanges may ultimately help to develop the basis for cooperation with the Soviet government within the larger framework of international relations and of the world community.

In addition to the growth of bilateral contacts under the cultural agreements with the U.S.S.R., the U.S. objective of developing greater communication between the Soviet people and ourselves is furthered through joint participation in the nonpolitical work of the United Nations and its specialized agencies. The membership of both the U.S.S.R. and the United States in the United Nations, Unesco, ILO, WHO, UPU, ITU, and WMO, and the involvement of Soviet and American personnel on the secretariats of those organizations, or in international conferences, or as technicians in the projects on health, education, science, humanities, meteorology, atomic energy development for peaceful uses, arid zone research, desalinization of water, telecommunications, etc., help to increase direct contact and communication between Russians and Americans. This may lead to somewhat greater mutual understanding of the respective ways of life, values, and objectives of the Communist and non-Communist peoples. It is to be hoped that these experiences will contribute to better political relations through the discovery of common technical interests and the experience of exchanging ideas. It is thus desirable for the United States to encourage participation by the U.S.S.R. in the U.N. agencies and to support programs within these agencies which will increasingly involve the Soviets in actual programs of international cooperation.[3]

Because of the rigid Soviet controls, private American organizations cannot get very far by themselves in developing cultural contacts with the Soviet Union. A similar situation prevails in other Communist countries. Government must, therefore, play a much larger part than in relations with non-Communist nations. Even when private groups participate, as they should, they need government aid and support. For example, when Benny Goodman and his orchestra visited the Soviet Union under the 1962 agreement the United States government had to be deeply involved in the details of arrangements with Goodman and in negotiating with the U.S.S.R. about dates, itinerary, the number of players in the orchestra, visas, and the like.

U.S. trade fairs and exhibits also illustrate the central role which the government must play in cultural relations with the U.S.S.R. The state-controlled Soviet economy, plus the fundamental ideological struggle between the Communists and ourselves, make these affairs highly significant political events. The products displayed are regarded as evidence of the quality and power of our nation—not merely of individual manufacturers. Any U.S. display becomes an expression of the American people, and so a potent influence on the image of the United States held by Soviet citizens. The size of the display, the nature of its contents, the quality of the U.S. personnel who explain the exhibits—all these affect the national interest, and must therefore be of concern to the federal government. Also the fairs and exhibits in which we participate are managed on the Soviet side exclusively by the government, to which a single American voice must be able to speak effectively. Moreover, the privilege of participating in Soviet fairs must be effectively related to the reciprocal privilege of the U.S.S.R. to participate in U.S. fairs—a task which only the government can perform with full grasp of the policy questions involved.

The reluctance of the Soviet government to recognize a distinction between private and governmental initiative on the U.S. side means that there must always be a high degree of cooperation between U.S. private agencies and the U.S. government. Despite the frustrations inevitable in dealing with Russia, the cooperation of private agencies is an essential feature of U.S. cultural action. For it shows that in our society the creative forces of education, science, technology, and the arts are free and not subject to governmental manipulation. They must, so far as possible, remain so even in relations with the U.S.S.R., in order to demonstrate to the Soviet people the vigor and variety of our society. Private efforts to develop cultural contacts with the Russians, encouraged where necessary but not managed or controlled by our government, provide an impressive demonstration of the place of education, science, and the arts in our kind of society. Our policy should be to permit professional groups such as the Inter-University Committee on Travel Grants, the American Council of Learned Societies, the National Academy of Sciences, and voluntary organizations such as the American Friends Service Committee to experiment with ways of establishing communication with the Soviet people. In doing this they may be making an important contribution to the foreign policy objectives of the United States.

The complexity of the task of relating the governmental and the private sectors in cultural relations with the Soviet Union is perhaps best illustrated by the so-called reciprocity issue that has plagued the cultural exchange program.

The United States, committed by its history and values to the idea that our interest is best served by the freest possible exchanges in education, science, the arts, technology, and information, has been confronted by Soviet hesitancy in allowing any exchanges, and obsession with maintaining strict reciprocity in whatever exchanges are arranged. We have not been inclined to keep score on who gains most from our exchanges with Western countries, and we have not followed the practice of making head-for-head reciprocity the condition of exchanges. It has been urged by some Americans that since the U.S.S.R. insists upon precise equivalence, we should be correspondingly rigid and demand exact reciprocal benefits for ourselves in return for what the Soviets get here. Thus if the Soviets wish us to admit certain scientists or industrialists to the United States for purposes important to them, we should insist on attaining objectives correspondingly important to us—securing access to Soviet archives for American scholars, for example. Others believe that we should always be ready to open doors and provide full freedom of access to others, including the Russians, thus demonstrating our belief in the concept of an open and free society.

The policy most consistent with U.S. commitments to freedom in thought, speech, and pursuit of knowledge is to avoid resort to reciprocity tactics wherever possible. We should refuse to let our own principles be corroded by emulating the U.S.S.R. in a policy consistent only with its totalitarian society. A wiser policy prevailed when this country, in July, 1962, extended the travel range of Soviet exchangees in this country without awaiting a *quid pro quo* extension of freedom of travel for American exchangees in the U.S.S.R.

When, however, it is clearly desirable to use the reciprocity policy in order to gain an important national objective, it may have to be employed.

The precautions taken by the Soviet government to control information about the United States that reaches the mass of its people require that special efforts be made in this field by the United States government. "If the public in countries controlled by dictatorships can exercise a moderating influence on its government officials," said Secretary of State Dean Rusk recently, "we must see to it that the public knows the facts. It must have more information than its governments are willing to make available."[4]

Almost the only effort that is presently feasible is short-wave radio broadcasting. The fact that the Soviet government employs about 2,000 jamming transmitters and spends about six times as much money trying to still the Voice of America as the broadcasts cost us is evidence that this is a significant medium for establishing contact with the mass of Soviet people.

It is impossible to evaluate after so short a time the impact of Soviet-American cultural exchanges upon individuals or upon government policies. United States participation in cultural relations with the U.S.S.R. is based upon faith in the power and effectiveness of ideas, whether these are stimulated by observation, conversation, reading, or other means. It is clear that Americans who have either acted as hosts to visiting Soviet citizens or have themselves visited the Soviet Union have acquired a much better insight into the nature and working of Soviet society. Their knowledge about the Soviet Union has been increased and they have been able to transmit much of it to large numbers of fellow Americans. We have gained knowledge about the state of Soviet science, technology, and research. We have had opportunities to observe Russian people at close range and in personal relationships. Unless one assumes that the people of the Soviet Union are a different breed of men, produced in the short space of 40 years since the Revolution, one must assume that their contacts with us have had similar effects. Indeed virtually all Americans who have seen Soviet citizens in contact with Americans and other foreigners have testified to the reality of this impact.[5]

U.S. policy toward the U.S.S.R. has two primary objectives. We seek first to withstand and counter the destructive aspects of Soviet foreign policy and to strengthen our defenses against their attacks upon democracy and the free world. We seek also to further such modifications of Soviet philosophy and policy as will make possible harmonious cooperation with them in the constructive efforts of the community of nations.

Cultural relations contribute to both of these objectives. The insights they make possible can provide the basis for a more realistic defense against aggression and, at the same time, assist in building bridges to the Soviet peoples, in developing limited experiences in cooperation under governmental sponsorship, and possibly in developing greater mutual confidence through such experiences.

COMMUNIST CHINA

Since the United States does not have diplomatic relations with the Communist government at Peiping, which controls continental China, there is no question of establishing formal educational, scientific, or other scholarly and artistic exchanges and there is no place for technical assistance at this stage of our relations. Nevertheless, the possibility of opening useful contacts, through public or private means, should be vigorously explored. Meantime, the Voice of America is the only cultural activity through which contact can be maintained. This assures an outside source of news to the small portion of the Chinese people who may have access to short-wave receivers. To these Chinese, and through them by word of mouth to countless others, it brings a reminder of the long history of cultural relations between China and the United States in science, education, technology and technical assistance, the arts and humanities, medicine, and religion. The Voice of America today beams seven and one-half hours daily of Chinese-language programs toward China.[6]

OTHER COMMUNIST COUNTRIES

Relations with the satellites present a mixed picture. In Poland there was a long tradition of cultural exchange with the United States, dating back to the early days of our independence. The heavy migration of Poles to this country provided a link that was hardly weakened until the Soviet-controlled government was established in

Warsaw. Until 1955 communication was significantly slowed, but since then there has been an increase in cultural contacts. These have included academic, scientific, and artistic exchanges. They are not based on a formal cultural agreement and consist on our side predominantly of private efforts, to which various educational and scientific bodies and foundations have contributed. The U.S. government has no libraries or cultural centers in Poland, but it did participate in the Poznan fair in June, 1962. The Voice of America broadcasts Polish-language programs for two hours daily; jamming is minimal and originates outside Poland. There are no U.S. government scientific or educational exchanges under Fulbright funds, but the Department of State has brought to this country groups of Polish journalists and some specialists for scientific congresses, and it has sent some Americans musical troupes to Poland. The United States maintains two cultural offices in Poland as compared with one in the U.S.S.R.

The absence of official bilateral programs and the still limited character of direct cultural relations between the United States and Poland gives to multilateral cultural relations a special importance. Since Poland is a member of all U.N. agencies except the Bank, the Fund, and the International Finance Corporation, Poles have become involved along with us in a wide range of cultural activities. These contribute to some extent to increasing the prospects for more general international cooperative relationships within the U.N. community. They also contribute to increasing the contacts of Poles with Americans in the professional and technical areas involved.

Among the Communist countries, Yugoslavia has been unique in the degree to which it has permitted the development of cultural relations with the United States. This is of special importance to our foreign policy objective of encouraging increasing independence by Yugoslavia in the conduct of its foreign relations, and in encouraging its full cooperation in the United Nations. Cultural activities, by developing stronger communications in scholarship, the arts, and technology, help to build up a community of professional interests among Yugoslavs and Americans that is fundamental to such an orientation in foreign relations. As with Russia, the central role of the Yugoslav government in cultural affairs makes it necessary for the U.S. government to play a central role in encouraging cultural cooperation, but it rightly emphasizes the private character of our cultural resources and must encourage private agencies, such as universities, in cooperative cultural enterprises with Yugoslavia. Here, too, the Voice of America must play an important part. Finally, since Yugoslavia is a member of all United Nations agencies except the International Finance Corporation, the government of the United States has many opportunities to strengthen understanding between the two countries by means of multilateral cultural cooperation.

Cultural relations have thus far played so insignificant a part in United States relations with Communist Czechoslovakia, Hungary, Rumania, and Bulgaria that they are hardly worth mentioning. There have been no technical assistance programs and virtually no exchanges, and the Voice of America has been the principal means of communication with these peoples. If and when their governments permit it, it will be to our advantage to develop the fullest possible opportunities for cultural exchange.

It has been emphasized that there is great variety among the Communist countries, reflected in degrees of rigidity in domestic controls and in attitudes toward each other and toward theoretical Marxian ideology. This variety provides opportunities for the United States, through cultural action, to develop communication and to convey a better knowledge of our own society and policies and of the United Nations concept of world community. In the absence of anything like normal diplomatic and trade relations, cultural relations represent the primary means of communication between ourselves and the people of most of these countries. Every useful opportunity afforded us should be seized and the advantage pressed to the utmost. Private agencies and the government share the responsibility for devising effective means for dealing with the complicated, frustrating, and often unpredictable systems of the totalitarian governments. There is a premium on experimentation, innovation, and risk-taking if we are to succeed in establishing connections with the Communist peoples, in relating their welfare to our own, and in increasing their involvement in the cooperative work of the world community.

UNDERDEVELOPED COUNTRIES

We have seen that cultural action is vitally important in U.S. relations with the Western, democratically-oriented countries and with the Communist countries. It plays an even more central role in the conduct of U.S. relations with the underdeveloped countries of Asia, Africa, Latin America, and the Middle East. This is because it is peculiarly relevant to the primary problems which face all these countries and which must be the primary concern of the United States in our policies toward them: their need for quickly developing more responsible and effective political systems for the conduct of both domestic and international affairs; their need for rapid progress in coping with the economic and social problems that threaten domestic stability and national survival; and their acute vulnerability to outside pressures—military, political, and ideological—from both Communist and non-Communist sources.

The need for more effective political systems arises in some instances from inexperience and from the fact that national states have only recently been created (as, for example, in the case of new African countries) or have only recently regained self-government (as in the case of some Asian countries). In others, the need arises from long delayed internal political development (as in most Latin American countries). In most newly developing countries, internal political instability and apparent unreadiness to participate freely, fully, and responsibly in world affairs provide the clearest evidence of their basic political needs. Most of them have not achieved an effectively responsible relationship between the people and the government. Even where the government appears to have general support, this often rests on unstable foundations.

The need of most of these countries for greatly accelerated progress in coping with economic and social problems is evident in the state of education, health and nutrition, agriculture, commerce and industry, and the professions, whether judged by absolute or by relative standards. Poverty, disease, malnutrition, and illiteracy constitute such formidable problems that internal stability and even independent national survival are threatened unless rapid progress can be made in dealing with them.

The acute vulnerability of most of the underdeveloped countries to outside pressures, military, political, and ideological, stems in part from their continued political, economic, and social instability. But it is greatly magnified by the strategic design of Communist aggression, which makes them the object of keen competitive attention by both Western and Communist countries.

It is clear that the primary objective of U.S. policy toward these countries must be to help them become politically stable, meet positively the social and economic demands of their citizens, resist Communist aggression, and participate constructively in world affairs. Our relations with them must be based on a high degree of mutual understanding and respect. Cultural activities provide the key ingredients both for assisting them in their developmental problems and for strengthening understanding with them. They are therefore the most critical component in U.S. relations with these countries.

DEVELOPMENT ASSISTANCE

Educational and scientific resources, which have provided the foundations for the advancement of all the more developed countries, constitute the most underdeveloped aspects of life in nearly all of the newly developing countries. The reason for this is to be found in large measure in the general isolation of the countries of Asia, Africa, the Middle East, and Latin America from the main stream of educational and scientific development that took place among Western nations during the last two centuries. The people of most of these areas were only peripherally involved in this essentially nongovernmental Western cooperative process. A notable exception was Japan, where a deliberate government program to acquire Western skills quickly brought the nation out of the underdeveloped category. Thailand's government financed extensive opportunities for foreign study designed to keep her abreast of Western developments. China became interested on its own initiative, and received help from other countries, including the United States government (Boxer Rebellion fund), and from many American private institutions. Within the framework of the British Empire, increasing numbers of persons in the colonies that were to become Pakistan, India, Ceylon, and Burma, and at a later stage those in certain African colonies, gradually became involved. This was partly due to private initiatives of universities and trading companies, but it was increasingly stimulated by British governmental efforts to train government personnel and to develop educational resources. French, Dutch, and Belgian colonies or spheres of influence were to some extent brought into the range of Western educational and scientific development. But even with all these local and external efforts the bulk of Asian, African, and Middle Eastern societies became only slightly involved in the dynamic Western intellectual developments of the eighteenth, nineteenth, and early twentieth centuries, or in the application of knowledge to the improvement of human welfare. Most Latin American countries maintained close intellectual ties across the Atlantic, but this was principally for the benefit of a very small elite. In only a few of these countries were the benefits of such contacts made the basis for general national development.

Because the educational and scientific resources of most countries in Africa, Asia, the Middle East, and Latin America do not provide in quantity, quality, or dynamism the foundations for economic, social, and political development, they need assistance across the broad spectrum of education, science, public administration, medicine, law, economics, agriculture, social service, business administration, and communications. They are lacking in qualified students, teachers, and research workers; in agricultural, industrial, health, and communications technicians; and in public administrators and experienced political leaders. They are, in short, lacking in the most essential manpower resources to get ahead quickly with their immense task of political, economic, and social development.

The magnitude and the urgency of what is required for fundamental cultural change are such that the necessary rapid progress cannot be achieved without substantial outside assistance. The slow evolutionary processes through which the Western countries achieved their modern levels of development will not suffice. Outside assistance must be on a large scale, of high quality, and assured for many decades to come. It must above all be carefully planned to fit actual needs.

The most fundamental kind of assistance needed is in the general realm of scientific and technical knowledge and education—in brief, in precisely the realm with which cultural relations are primarily concerned. It is for this reason that cultural activities are so important to the conduct of U.S. relations with the underdeveloped countries.

The resources for assistance are of course not limited to what the United States can provide. Many other countries, especially in recent years as their economies have recovered from war-time collapse or dislocation, have heeded the demands of the newly developing areas. Much of this help has come through United Nations agencies, supported by member states. Some of it has come through assistance programs continued from colonial administration by the United Kingdom and France, or provided directly by private and governmental sources from many nations including the Scandinavian countries, Canada, Israel, Germany, Japan, the U.S.S.R., and Communist China. The Colombo Plan and the new Aid Group of the OECD have stimulated and coordinated individual national efforts.

Nor are the resources for U.S. development assistance through cultural action limited to those provided by the government. Many private groups—churches, foundations, universities, business firms, and service organizations—as well as individuals have in the past contributed substantially toward modernization in many underdeveloped areas. Since the rush to independence after World War II, these private efforts have markedly increased. They have helped to develop educational and scientific institutions in Asia, Africa, and Latin America. They have brought to the United States for education and training large numbers of scholars, teachers, research workers, technicians, businessmen, and public officials. They have sent to the underdeveloped countries large numbers, as well, of American specialists and technicians. The bulk of undergraduates in American colleges and universities from less developed countries have come with private financing, including that provided by their own families.

In short, the present role of the U.S. governmental cultural relations program as it relates to the needs of the underdeveloped areas must be seen in the context of both the non-American and the very substantial private American efforts; it should complement these other efforts in its pursuit of U.S. foreign policy objectives.

U.S. governmental assistance through cultural activities must also be effectively related to other kinds of assistance, such as the providing of loans and equipment. The development of skills and competence in the broadest sense, which is promoted by cultural activities, is only a part of the total developmental process.

The kind of government cultural programs needed to serve the foreign policy objectives of the U.S. in relation to the undeveloped countries has emerged fairly clearly as a result of many years of experience since World War II.

What is required is a composite of activities that contribute both to the immediate education and training of a wide variety of *people* and to the development of *institutions* through which the less developed countries can themselves provide education and training. The persons to be reached immediately through outside assistance include teachers, research workers, and technicians at various levels in all the professions—education, medicine, engineering, law, agriculture, social welfare, business, public administration. The institutions needing development are at all levels of the formal educational process—primary, secondary, collegiate, post graduate—and include also research and training centers outside the formal educational system, such as agricultural experiment stations, hospitals and medical laboratories, and technological research institutions. Besides activities that help in the immediate education or training of people and the development of educational institutions, there is need to encourage the growth of transnational professional relationships in education, science, the arts, and technology, like the contacts that underlie our relations with Western countries. Finally, the cultural program should contribute to the development of modernized economies, dynamic social systems, and responsible governments—that is, to institutional development in the broadest sense.

The objectives of cultural relations with underdeveloped countries, it will be seen, are enormously more complex than those of programs with either Western or Communist countries. If these activities are to play their central role in the conduct of U.S. relations with underdeveloped countries, they must be interrelated and coordinated to assure that all of them make their full contribution to these complex objectives. Each exchange of students, teachers, research workers, and scholars, each dispatch of technicians, and each arriving delegation of civilian or military participants for training in the United States must be seen as a calculated commitment of funds or personnel to help achieve desirable changes in the country concerned. This implies, of course, a development plan worked out by the country itself and a matching country plan of the United States for development assistance. It implies also a clear determination of the character and extent of the American effort in relation to assistance from other countries or through mutilateral means such as the U.N., the Colombo Plan, or the Development Assistance Group in the OECD.

STRENGTHENING UNDERSTANDING

The promotion of mutual understanding is the other major contribution that cultural activities can make to U.S. relations with underdeveloped countries. Mutual understanding cannot be taken for granted; it will not come about by itself without special effort. We must be aware of important influences in our relations with these countries, some favorable and some unfavorable to understanding and hence to effective cooperation in the free world community. Cultural activities can strengthen the first and mitigate the second.

A favorable factor is the high prestige that the United States enjoys as a former colony that has successfully developed under a democratic system into a prosperous and powerful nation. Many national independence movements, as their leaders readily attest, relied heavily upon American experience and constitutional doctrines or borrowed from the same sources from which we have borrowed. It is recognized that the United States has usually behaved sympathetically and generously toward independence movements, and has been disposed to help the newly independent countries to achieve their goals. There is relatively little doubt about our basic democratic orientation, and our commitment to the rule of law and to the observance of human rights. Many of the newest constitutions—for example those of Guinea, Nigeria, Ivory Coast, Madagascar, Tunisia, Republic of the Congo, Libya, Cameroon, Senegal—include language about human rights very similar to that of our own. We are known as a nation whose prosperity is broadly based on an essentially classless society. Increasing numbers of Americans have developed close personal and professional ties with the people of the underdeveloped areas. The products of the American economy and culture are in great demand.

Working against these positive factors are several negative elements, some of modern origin, others stemming from earlier times. In the setting of complex world tensions these often seem to have greater influence than the positive factors.

In all of the underdeveloped regions recent years have seen a great increase in Communist propaganda from the U.S.S.R. and from Communist China. This is designed to discredit the role of the West, including the United States, in international affairs, to cast doubt on the disinterestedness of American intentions toward the underdeveloped countries, and to persuade the latter that their best hope rests in association with the Communist side in the world struggle.

A second negative element has been the association of the United States with Western colonial and ex-colonial powers. We have noted that for the survival and growth of the free world community, nothing is of more crucial importance than the close ties that exist between the United States and the nations of western Europe. Nevertheless, the same ties have frequently constituted a serious handicap in our relations with the newly independent countries. They have served to associate us, in the minds of their peoples, with past colonial domination and with the resistance to independence movements shown by countries such as France and Portugal. Great strains have developed in U.S. relations with both the new countries and the Western countries as we have attempted to honor our traditional commitment to self-determination and political freedom as well as our commitment to our Western allies, with whom we share responsibility for resisting Communist aggression, both against ourselves and against newly developing countries. We are caught in the conflicting values of a disappearing world order and an emerging world order more consistent with the modern national independence movements.

A third and related barrier to effective cooperation has been the unpleasant reputation of the United States resulting from its past policies in Latin America. There is much in the record to justify the distrust and fear of our intentions found today in Latin America and elsewhere. Citizens of the United States have been associated in many Latin American countries with domestic economic exploitation and with corrupt and dictatorial governments. During much of the history of our relations with our southern neighbors we have displayed arrogance and other attitudes characteristic of some colonial powers toward less developed peoples. Latin American economies have too often been controlled from the United States much as colonial empires were controlled from the metropolitan country. The American government, though seldom exercising direct political control, has at times intervened to make possible highly profitable private U.S. investments, leaving to chance the impact, good or bad, which these investments might have on the economic and political life of the country in question. A United States attitude of understanding, concern, and cooperation and a positive search for means to achieve common goals of the peoples of the Western hemisphere have been until recently the exception rather than the rule. The pro-Castro sentiment in many parts of Latin America has been probably less an endorsement of Communism than an indictment of our generally inept policies toward Latin America as a whole.

A fourth negative factor influencing the prospects for understanding is the very prosperity and power of the United States, which are almost incomprehensible when seen from the viewpoint of the staggeringly poor populations of underdeveloped countries. It is, of course, precisely our wealth and power that provide the means of assisting these countries, but the differences between them and ourselves are so great that they often hinder effective cooperation toward common goals. Nowhere is this better illustrated than in the cliché long current in some Asian countries that contrasts the alleged "materialism" of the United States with the alleged "spirituality" of the non-Western countries—a formula that may satisfy the national ego but that is neither justified in fact nor conducive to full cooperation.

Each of these negative factors to some extent affects U.S. relations with all the underdeveloped countries. They tend often to outweigh the many positive influences that should facilitate cooperation between us. The negative factors have been influential because of the absence in our relations with these countries of any real sense of community based on common values and experiences, such as today provides the foundation for cooperation between the United States and the Western countries.

In many respects cultural activities of the U.S. government in the course of development assistance are the most important single factor today promoting understanding between ourselves and the developing countries. By such means we identify ourselves with the social, political, and economic revolution that is altering the lives of hundreds of millions of people. The manner in which this assistance is administered of course largely determines its effectiveness. The widespread personal contacts that such activities entail between the people of these countries and Americans, both overseas and in the United States, reveal more about us and our values than the dollars we spend or the official words we use to explain our actions.

There are, nevertheless, government cultural activities that are designed more directly to promote mutual understanding with the underdeveloped countries. These include substantially the same types of program that are used in Western and in Communist countries, though their focus and magnitude necessarily differ. They include libraries and information centers, leader and specialist grants, English-language training, promotion of American studies, the Voice of America, and other mass media activities and cultural presentations. Others involve cooperative action through the U.N. or other international organizations.

Libraries and information centers, here as elsewhere, provide a picture of the United States. They are especially needed in the underdeveloped countries, whose people have had few contacts with the United States, know little about us, and have few sources of information. Because their educational institutions and mass media are largely underdeveloped, an extraordinary effort is required to bring to these people an image of the United States that approaches factual reality. The steady flow of people into these information centers and the demand for books and other reading matter about the United States reveal the major contribution that both the libraries and the centers are capable of making toward increasing understanding. In addition they often serve as important substitutes for nonexistent national library resources on education, engineering, science, technology, history, politics, and government. Since they are established not only in the big cities but also in places accessible only by truck, caravan, or river boat, their influence goes well beyond urban populations and can reach far out into rural areas.

A significant contribution to understanding is made by the government's program to increase the distribution of American books in the underdeveloped countries. This program, through which American books are made available in translation at prices ordinary people can afford, is particularly important in view of the flood of low-cost books issuing from the U.S.S.R. and Communist China.

The English-language teaching program is much more important in the underdeveloped countries than in the West, not only because it increases the number of persons with whom we can communicate directly, but also because in many multilingual countries English is coming to be the one common national language. Moreover, the English language offers direct access to much of the content of modern Western culture and technology not yet available in translation, and indeed often untranslatable into the vocabularies of the underdeveloped countries. While most of these countries are placing more emphasis upon English-language instruction in their schools, very few have the facilities or experience to achieve rapid progress in this respect unless they happen to have benefited previously from the teaching of English as a second language under a colonial administration.

American studies programs, it will be recalled, have been successful in Europe. They are also important as a means of encouraging a deeper background of understanding in the countries of Asia, Africa, the Middle East, and Latin America. They are an important counterpart to the intensive development of non-Western studies now going on in the United States. Government programs to develop channels of communication through mass media are also of special importance in underdeveloped countries. They present immensely complicated and often costly problems, largely due to the underdeveloped state of the media themselves. It is often necessary to train journalists and radio and motion picture technicians as well as to provide news about the United States and a wide range of feature services.

The fine arts, drama, music, and literature likewise play a special role in our relations with the countries of the Middle East, Africa, Latin America, and Asia. Traditionally, most of the contacts in these fields between the countries of these regions and the West have been with Europe. As a result, the achievements of the United States in the arts remain largely unknown. The so-called President's cultural presentation program has made it possible for symphony orchestras, theater companies, and individual artists from the United States to go on extended tours in the underdeveloped countries. Until suitable commercial or other private facilities have developed to assure non-governmental arrangements for such visits, it is desirable to continue them under government auspices.

Finally, cultural action through United Nations agencies significantly furthers mutual understanding between the United States and the underdeveloped countries. Most important are the development assistance programs in education, health, nutrition, agriculture, and social welfare, notably under the Expanded Program of Technical Assistance and the Special Fund. Our participation in these joint efforts of the world community not only associates us with the tasks upon which the underdeveloped countries are embarked, but reveals to them the disinterestedness of our own concern in that we make contributions to programs in which control is shared by many countries.

The efforts of Unesco to increase international understanding, especially through research and through conferences on such topics as the values and character of Western and non-Western cultures, provide a multilateral approach with which we should continue to be deeply involved. The focus of Unesco's effort has been upon increasing exchanges of knowledge concerning the music, literature, and philosophy of various regions and upon the more systematic study of societies, especially in the non-Western countries. These efforts to further mutual understanding and more effective cooperation within the world community have had sustained support from both Western and non-Western countries.

It has been suggested that the role of cultural activities is even more central in the conduct of relations with underdeveloped countries than in relations with the West and with Communist states. With Western countries a governmental cultural program reinforces traditional relationships and strengthens the basis for cooperative action in international affairs. With Communist countries it provides the principal means for overcoming the barriers imposed by totalitarian governments and for developing a basis of communication between the American people and the Communist peoples. But with underdeveloped countries cultural activities are at once the principal means for attaining primary substantive objectives of U.S. foreign policy and for creating a climate in which these objectives can be achieved.

Hence the various kinds of cultural activities in the conduct of U.S. relations with the underdeveloped countries must be seen as an integrated whole rather than as separate segments. Programs of technical assistance for the development of higher or secondary educational systems, or for improving agricultural productivity by training technicians and establishing agricultural experiment stations, or for introducing mechanized processes in place of hand work in various kinds of industry, or for improving health and nutritional services, or for professionalizing the service of public administration —all such programs are concerned with the task of achieving change through the development of more competent human resources. They all are basically of an educational character. They all involve personal, face-to-face cooperation and are thus an excellent means of developing understanding between peoples. They are all basic to social, economic, and political development. Information centers and libraries, educational exchanges, mass media activities, and cultural presentations are also inseparable parts of the total effort, not only because they too are basically educational, but because they help directly in developing a more favorable climate of understanding. All these activities help to strengthen the developing countries for participation in the free world community.

Not the least important aspect of the cultural relations program is its effect upon the people of the United States. By broadening our knowledge and experience of the great awakening continents of Asia, Africa, and Latin America we are fitting ourselves to play more wisely and more effectively a role of leadership in the free world community.

It has been the thesis of this chapter that transnational cultural activities are important to the conduct of U.S. foreign relations because they contribute to the advancement of knowledge, to economic, social, and political growth, to the development of understanding, and to the promotion of a sense of world community.

In our relations with Western countries, cultural relations are an essential means for promoting common objectives. With Communist countries, cultural relations are the most hopeful means for introducing ventilating currents and laying the basic foundations for understanding. With underdeveloped countries, cultural relations provide

184 The Role of Cultural Activities

the principal means of helping to modernize their societies in the context of a strong, voluntary world order.

So basic and essential are these contributions to the pursuit of U.S. foreign policy objectives in the present state of world affairs that concern with the adequacy of cultural relations must be a continuing, major preoccupation of the U.S. government. The concluding chapter will discuss some of the requisites for governmental effectiveness in giving expression to its concern.

SEVEN

Toward an
Effective Cultural Program

THE OVERRIDING aim of American foreign policy is the
building of a cohesive and peaceful world community based on consent. This aim can be significantly advanced by an intensive, long-
range program of cultural exchanges. Cooperative efforts with other
countries to (1) enlarge the boundaries of human knowledge, (2)
apply existing knowledge to the advancement of human welfare, and
(3) create mutual appreciation among peoples of different cultural
backgrounds are desirable in themselves. They will also, in many
important ways, help to create a world community in which free institutions can survive. Cultural relations should therefore be a major dimension in the conduct of United States foreign relations.

Under what conditions can the cultural relations program of the
United States government realize its immense possibilities for positive, constructive achievement?

It is not necessary to examine in detail the operational experience
of the last quarter century to find the answer. Conversations with
government officials and friendly citizens of many countries in Asia,
the Middle East, Europe, and Latin America confirm the judgments
of many of our own officials and private citizens about the reasons
why some cultural programs succeed and others fail. If the total impact of our national effort has been less than it should have been, the

185

reason is not simply a matter of size or cost of the program. The effectiveness of cultural action depends upon many factors, among which the following seem most important and are directly within our own power to control or correct.

1. *The central importance of cultural action must be recognized.* The cultural relations program must have its spokesmen at the heart of the policy-making process. It must be taken into account in the daily conduct of foreign relations at all levels, from the President down to the youngest vice consul or desk officer in the Department of State. Its importance must be fully understood by the Congress and by the public at large.

The technical assistance component of cultural relations is beginning, but only beginning, to be thus recognized. It was long considered a mere appendage of economic or military assistance. Even now it is widely looked upon as a temporary concern of the U.S. government rather than as a continuing central preoccupation for decades to come. In the information field, even those activities that contribute directly to cold war propaganda receive reluctant support from Congress, while libraries and information centers are easy victims when over-all budget ceilings call for economies. Educational and scientific exchanges as well as those in the arts ordinarily have low priority in State Department and Congressional budget decisions. In planning and administering our relations with individual countries, cultural activities such as technical aid, information, and educational exchange have too often been considered as separate from each other and as accessory, rather than as an integral part coordinate in importance with the economic and the political.

In spite of improvements in the Fulbright-Hays Act and the Act for International Development, the total cultural relations program remains segmented, poorly coordinated, and inadequately financed. In sharp contrast to the treatment accorded to military programs, Congressional discussion of cultural relations is usually concerned mainly with cutting costs, and legislators are loath to approve budgets unless quick and visible results can be guaranteed. Experimental military programs that commit billions of dollars for the development of a single new bomber program, for a new missile or submarine are readily authorized, but a modest increase of a few millions for the total cultural program is subjected to minute critical examination, conducted in an atmosphere of extreme skepticism and even hostility.

If the full possibilities of a cultural relations program are to be realized, much more determined leadership on the highest level is imperative. The President and the Secretary of State must not only vigorously champion such a program, as is now increasingly the case, but they must also somehow compel serious attention to it at all levels of the bureaucracy. Congress must understand its importance and give much more than the halting support that emerges from the tortuous processes of legislative committees. The public must be aware of this new dimension in foreign policy and demand of both the President and the Congress a sound program adequately financed and centrally geared to foreign policy needs. Only thus can the far-reaching potential of the cultural relations dimension be realized.

2. *Sound governmental organization and administrative procedures are required.* The basic elements for this are easily stated. Under presidential leadership, the Secretary of State must have the power to relate the planning and operations of all the different kinds of governmental cultural activities to United States policy in individual countries and in international organizations.

This goal is more easily stated than attained. The bulk of these activities are now concentrated under the direction of the U.S. Information Agency, the Agency for International Development, and the Bureau of Educational and Cultural Affairs in the Department of State. They entail the cooperation of nearly 20 other federal agencies as well, including the Departments of Labor, Agriculture, Defense, and Health, Education and Welfare. Each of these agencies should, in its own area, make its contribution to this aspect of foreign policy. Although there is fortunately only one Secretary of State in Washington and one principal American diplomatic representative in each country and at the U.N., the bulge of bureaucracy between them is so immense that the achievement of coordinated action by the many agencies and bureaus toward clearly defined foreign policy objectives requires the most extraordinary and persistent efforts. Such coordination has not been achieved to date. The program of the United States in any one country has reflected not so much a rational appraisal of the actual needs and opportunities in that country as an adding together of activities that happened to fall within the budgetary responsibilities of different agencies.

Below the Secretary of State, no official has been able to compel the injection of the full range of cultural relations into policy planning and administration or to achieve coordination among even the three principal competing bureaucracies (State, USIA, and AID). There is an Assistant Secretary of State for Educational and Cultural Affairs, who ranks with all the many other Assistant Secretaries for geographic regions and miscellaneous other functions. He competes with them for funds in the budget processes of the Department of State and of the Executive Branch as well as before the Congress. He himself is in charge of one of the competing bureaucracies to be coordinated. At the embassies abroad, personnel who are to carry out his part of the cultural program are under the direction of the principal USIA officer.

Within the Department of State, the authority to coordinate the work of all agencies must be at a level equivalent to that at which the economic aspects of foreign policy are concerted. If the latter is at the level of an under-secretary, as was the case early in 1962, the assignment of a lower rank for the coordination of cultural action makes an invidious distinction and makes less effective the role of the Department of State in relation to other agencies.

3. *There must be an effective working relationship between government and private efforts.* Our national vitality and strength derive in large part from the way our particular combination of pluralism and democracy encourages private and governmental activities to complement each other. The relationship between the two is a matter of continuing adjustment rather than a rigid, systematic pattern.

Traditionally, in the United States, educational, scientific, technological, and artistic cooperation with other countries, as well as communication through mass media, has rested upon private initiative. Only recently has the government become systematically involved in such matters; during most of its history its role has been largely passive. Because of our emphasis upon individualism and private enterprise, U.S. educational and scientific agencies operating abroad have tended to be jealous of their independence. It is still widely believed that if a private organization accepts government advice or guidance, or if the government calls attention to foreign policy considerations, the unique values of private activity are in danger of erosion. Fears are expressed that any deviation from purely professional motivations would subvert that freedom of individual decision that is our proudest boast. There is much evidence that foreign governments and professional groups are far less suspicious of cultural action when it is carried on by private agencies than when it is operated by the U.S. government.

Government, however, became involved in transnational cultural activities because of very real national needs and not through arbitrary intervention. These needs grew out of the expanding participation of the American people in world affairs and the demands of foreign policy. Government alone can speak for all the people in such matters as negotiating cultural agreements or planning technical assistance, and only government can provide the leadership to identify national goals and to allocate national resources necessary to the promotion of these goals. Government also is the appropriate agency to decide whether private cultural activities promote or endanger the national interest. Government is uniquely situated to observe the ways in which our multiple efforts are interrelated and how they might be made more effective. It can see the relation of short-term and long-term goals, of various private and government efforts. It can encourage private initiative and identify areas where such initiative is most needed. It can identify means for relating U.S. private and governmental efforts to those of other countries.

The private and public sectors in cultural relations can work together only if there are easy means for continuing consultation and cooperative planning. The government agencies must be so organized and administered that responsible discussion can take place with private agencies, both abroad and in Washington. This kind of organization has still not been sufficiently developed.

The nongovernmental agencies, in turn, must be sensitive to the foreign policy implications of cultural relations and willing to consult with government so that the national interest may always be furthered.* The multiplicity and variety of these agencies, including

* For example, a self-imposed embargo by the motion picture industry of the United States on the exportation of low-grade pictures that misrepresent American life and undermine our reputation and prestige abroad would be one of the most important contributions that could be made to the achievement of U.S. foreign policy objectives and would significantly reinforce the cultural action of the government.

universities, professional associations, foundations, business organizations, churches, and other voluntary groups engaged in cultural activities abroad make responsible consultation difficult, but it would be a mistake to attempt any consolidation or coordination of the private sector that endangered the pluralism that is part of our national strength.[1]

The cooperative arrangements found in the Fulbright program, exchanges with the U.S.S.R., and university technical assistance contracts illustrate how the public and private sectors can work together. Where government and private efforts are in a kind of partnership, it is of paramount importance that the arrangements allow the private agencies the freedom to make their unique contributions in their own way, with government supervision limited to necessary political guidance. The history of university contracts in technical assistance, for example, shows the continuing tendency of government agencies to limit so rigidly the exercise of professional judgment and to surround university operations by such a network of administrative regulations that the real advantages of university involvement in cultural action are not attained.[2] The making of grants to universities, as is done by foundations, would be preferable to the contract mechanism, which is suitable for controlling the delivery of materials or the building of highways but is far less appropriate in essentially long-term educational ventures.

An important aspect of the relationship between government and private efforts concerns the role of international nongovernmental organizations, such as the International Council of Scientific Unions, the International Association of Universities, or the International Institute of Administrative Sciences in developing transnational cultural cooperation. Representing private voluntary groups in education, science, technology, the arts, and information, these bodies form a part of the slowly growing framework of the world community. The strengthening of these organizations through financial and other forms of support is consistent with our support of private cooperation and serves to bring to our cultural program many of the benefits associated with international cooperation.

4. *Cultural activities should aim at genuine cooperation with other countries* and not merely unilateral action of which others are the object or beneficiary. Shared goals and responsibilities make for

stronger commitments and mutual respect. Many of the broader objectives of our foreign policy are shared by other peoples, and some have been defined as common goals in the charters of the United Nations agencies and in regional organizational commitments. A positive policy of collaboration with other countries, making them donors as well as recipients, strengthens our national efforts.

Where cultural activities are organized on a bilateral basis, mutuality of interest should be emphasized. This approach undoubtedly enhanced the reputation of the Fulbright program, which frankly recognized that reciprocal efforts are necessary to achieve international understanding. (Its new legislative form, significantly, is entitled "Mutual Educational and Cultural Exchange Act.") In its earlier stages, the Point Four technical assistance program appealed to the underdeveloped countries because it was seen as a plan for economic cooperation with recognized mutual benefits. At some later stages, U.S. technical assistance appeared to many countries to be identified with political arm-twisting and the development of military alliances. Even under the relatively new Alliance for Progress Latin American countries have questioned whether, in fact, joint planning will prevail or whether the program will be "made in U.S.A." Information programs often have had an unhappy one-sidedness, verging on mere propaganda or cheap advertising.

Whenever practicable, United States cultural efforts should be carried on through the United Nations, WHO, IAO, Unesco, ILO, and other multilateral associations both universal and regional. This procedure underlines the universality of the values we seek to promote and the genuineness of our commitment to these values. The multilateral approach helps reduce frictions that inevitably come from the fact of our size and the disproportionate role of world leadership we must assume, and encourages other nations to identify themselves with the successes or failures of our joint efforts. It reduces the danger of political control. It emphasizes the reciprocal benefits to be achieved by cooperation. It militates against competition and overlapping efforts as more countries contribute assistance to the newly developing lands. It increases the likelihood of persuading other developed countries to reduce the burden on the United States by increasing their own contributions to international assistance programs. Finally, the U.N. agencies, like private international associations, are part of the framework of world community that we seek to strengthen.

5. *An effective cultural relations program must be imaginatively planned and flexibly administered.* Cultural activities are mainly creative efforts, and they involve us with the creative elements in other societies. Therefore a cultural relations program must itself be creative, flexible, and responsive to the needs of the particular country in which it operates. There can be few stereotypes or blueprinted standard programs, because countries differ and so do the people within them.

Flexibility in planning and administering cultural programs is also necessary to permit reaching different groups of people within countries. We think of ourselves as a dynamic people moving forward to realize the benefits of a free and democratic society. We must, therefore, develop programs that relate us to the aspirations of people in other countries, including sometimes the discontented, the anti-American, the left-of-center, and the emerging youth groups, who may be similarly thinking and building toward a better society.

All of this means that the total cultural relations program undertaken by the United States with each country must, in its content, balance, and magnitude, meet the special needs of our relations with that individual country. This requires careful country planning of all the elements that go into a total cultural program. Such country planning has not as yet been achieved by the agencies concerned.

The tendency of bureaucratic patterns to harden in terms of old categories of programs, work habits, and personnel is a major barrier to achieving flexibility. Equally harmful is the habitual practice in the Congressional appropriation process of focusing upon issues that are likely to embarrass the executive agencies, and upon making a record of having cut the budget request of the executive, even at the expense of endangering national objectives.

6. *A cultural relations program must deliberately seek to develop among the American people an awareness of the world community and a commitment to it.* It must be seen as the inevitable international dimension of the cultural life of the American people. Its purpose should be as much to relate the people of the United States effectively to the world community of the arts, sciences, technology, and education as it is to relate other people to the kind of world we

prefer. Understanding by the American people of our world responsibilities and of foreign cultures and institutions should be as much the objective of government cultural action programs as is the promotion of understanding by others. Far too little emphasis is placed today in the U.S. cultural program upon educating ourselves. The program is still primarily outward oriented.

7. *A fundamental need is continuing research on the processes of communication that lie at the heart of cultural relations,* and on the processes by which the world community may be achieved. A substantially larger amount in each year's appropriation should be devoted to research in this field. We should know more accurately the factors that make for successful educational exchange experiences. The technical assistance process, involving the transfer of skills and ideas across cultural barriers, is so complicated that we are still guessing in much of what we do to provide assistance to other countries. The actual impact of many of our information activities is still not objectively established. This is an area in which the universities can continue to make a major contribution to national policy and program development.

8. *Constancy and sufficient magnitude are essential.* Crash programs may do more harm than good in cultural relations, and long-term objectives cannot be attained without long-term commitments of adequate scope. In our relations with Latin America today we see both the inadequacy and the dangers of our "off again, on again" cultural policies toward this area in the last 30 years. We now risk repeating this story in Europe, where the admirable beginnings made during the last 15 years are being jeopardized by a shifting of funds to new areas regarded as strategically more important—the assumption being that political relations with Western countries already rest on solid foundations, and that cultural relations programs with "friends" are an expendable luxury. This assumption is false. Even in Europe, only a constant program continuing steadily over many decades can assure the kind of relationships upon which our joint leadership in the world community depends. What is needed is an increase in funds sufficient both to maintain the Western programs and to add whatever new programs are necessary to meet our new responsibilities elsewhere, as in Africa and southeast Asia.

We also risk repeating our earlier errors in thinking that developmental objectives sought through educational processes can be achieved by quick exposures or spray-gun techniques. If we are in earnest about our goals in newly developing countries, we must be ready to commit ourselves for periods of twenty years or longer.

Because of the importance of cultural action as a major dimension of foreign relations, its magnitude must be sufficient to enable it to make its fullest possible contribution. Small-scale, marginal programs can become irritants and cause frustration and disappointment. The long-range nature of many tasks does not mean that the time span available is unlimited. While mutual understanding among nations must inevitably grow slowly, the urgent need for it requires that the process be speeded by every conceivable means. Educational development is at best a slow process, but every effort should be made to quicken its pace. Modernization of nations, delayed by many historic factors, must proceed with maximum speed. Long-term commitments, and the largest feasible magnitude of effort, are absolute requisites for an effective cultural relations program.

9. *The program must be of first-rate quality in both content and personnel.* This factor is perhaps more important than any other. Inferior programs will merely cheapen us in the eyes of the world, and money spent on them will be worse than wasted. Personnel who are badly chosen, poorly briefed, and too frequently transferred from post to post cannot fairly represent the United States. Persons going abroad to provide technical assistance, whether they are selected by government or by private agencies, must be representative of the best in our society and not merely the most readily available or the least costly. In no other aspect of U.S. representation abroad is our prestige so much involved in the individual who represents us.

Poorly planned exchanges, inferior cultural presentations, or cheap advertising techniques in information programs not only fail to advance our national objectives but positively harm the reputation of the United States abroad.* They provide useful ammunition for our enemies, and they undermine the confidence of our friends.

* Foreigners often express a preference for the news reporting of the BBC (British Broadcasting Corporation) over that of the Voice of America and the U.S. Armed Services Network. The phrenetic and ultra-dramatic style of news broadcasting in the United States is unacceptable to many other people. Quality in performance here requires a careful regard for objectivity and a calm, matter-of-fact manner of reporting.

Essential to the maintenance of program quality abroad is the mobilization at home of people of the highest professional competence to advise and consult with the government and to take on program responsibilities. In three fields (exchange of persons, information, and Unesco relations) the government has experimented with the device of permanent advisory commissions, with varied functions and with considerably varying degrees of effectiveness. The Board of Foreign Scholarships (Fulbright program) represents a different way of mobilizing professional competence, in this case for operational rather than merely advisory services. Contracts with universities and other professional institutions represent, in part, an effort to assure quality in the area of technical assistance.

Continuing attention has been given to the development of governmental career services, and of means by which to bring high-level professional personnel temporarily into various kinds of cultural relations programs. Progress in this respect, however, has been slow because of continuing uncertainties about the long-term role of cultural action in U.S. foreign policy.

Within the short space of twenty-five years a wholly new dimension has entered into the conduct of U.S. foreign relations. Firmly based upon a foundation of nongovernmental cultural cooperation across international boundaries, government cultural action through education, science, the arts, information, and technical assistance has emerged as a major resource for the achievement of long-term foreign policy objectives. Its contribution is increasingly effective in relations with Western, Communist, and newly developing countries.

Cultural activities are not instruments capable of affecting the immediate maintenance of peace. This depends on the intelligent use of other dimensions in the conduct of international relations. The cultural dimension, however, is indispensable as a longer-range means of creating the genuine world community of values and experience that our ever-growing interdependence requires. The imaginative, purposeful development of this dynamic new dimension therefore presents a challenge of major significance to both the government and the people of the United States.

Notes

CHAPTER ONE—THE PURPOSE OF THIS BOOK

1. Summarized from Edward R. Murrow, address before the Annual Conference of the American Association of Industrial Educators, New York, April 5, 1962. USIA release no. 23, Washington, D.C.

2. "Assignment USA," *Indiana University Bulletin,* Vol. LX, No. 11 (May 15, 1962).

3. U.S. Department of State, *Educational and Cultural Diplomacy, 1961* (Washington, 1962), p. 65.

4. AID, "Summary of Health Programs," background paper for Ninth Annual Meeting of the National Conference on International Economics and Social Development, Chicago, Ill., July 19–20, 1962.

5. Interim report on the implementation of the 1961–62 program, in Annual Report of the Technical Assistance Board, United Nations Economic and Social Council, Official Records: 34th sess., Supplement no. 5 (New York, 1962).

CHAPTER TWO—THE BEGINNINGS: 1938–1945

1. For an annotated classification of the treaties, resolutions, and recommendations adopted at Inter-American Conferences and Meetings of Consultation up to 1956, on political, economic, social, and cultural subjects, including technical cooperation, see *Manual of Inter-American Relations,* revised (Washington: Pan American Union, 1956).

2. *Report of the Delegation of the United States of America to the*

Inter-American Conference for the Maintenance of Peace, Buenos Aires, December 1–23, 1936 (Washington, 1937), p. 34. For the text of the Convention see *Treaty Information,* Bulletin No. 89, February, 1937 (Washington: Government Printing Office, 1937), pp. 29–31. The Convention was revised at Caracas in 1954, and for this text, together with a summary, see *Department of State Bulletin,* 1956, 34:176–80. The original Convention was eventually ratified by 17 nations; the Convention as revised at Caracas, by 7 (as of January 1, 1962). Department of State, *Treaties in Force* (Washington, 1962).

3. *Government Programs in International Education,* Forty-Second Report by the Committee on Government Operations, House Report No. 2712, 85th Cong., 2d sess. (1959), pp. 33–34.

4. *Harvard Graduates' Magazine,* 1900–1901, 9:37–43.

5. I. L. Kandel, *United States Activities in International Cultural Relations* (Washington: American Council on Education, 1945), pp. 80–82.

6. James R. Mock and Cedric Larson, *Words That Won the War* (Princeton: Princeton University Press, 1939), p. 331.

7. On the development of national programs of cultural relations see Ruth E. McMurry and Muna Lee, *The Cultural Approach* (Chapel Hill: University of North Carolina Press, 1947).

8. For a world review of the distribution of means of mass communication see Unesco, *World Communications,* 3rd ed. (Paris: Unesco, 1956).

9. A resident of Buenos Aires, Argentina, who ordered books on Lincoln and Washington from a New York publisher was asked if he could call for his package at one of several cities in Brazil. Harry Erwin Bard, *Intellectual and Cultural Relations Between the United States and the Other Republics of America* (Washington: Carnegie Endowment for International Peace, 1914), p. 23.

10. Assistant Secretary of State George S. Messersmith, testifying in May, 1938, before the House Committee on Appropriations on the establishment of the Division of Cultural Relations, spoke of "information from Brazil, from the Argentine, from Peru, in fact from most of the countries of South America, that certain governments are pressing on them professors and students and professional and technical advisors of various kinds." Such activities were "causing serious damage to our interests and prestige there." They had been carried forward to "such alarming degree" as to create a situation which was "a matter of major as well as of immediate importance." *Second Deficiency Appropriation Bill for 1938,* House,

Committee on Appropriations, 75th Cong., 3d sess. (1938), pp. 654–57.

11. Its name was changed in December, 1944, to Interdepartmental Committee on Cultural and Scientific Cooperation.

12. For the text of Public Law 355, see 53 Stat. 1290 (1939), 7 U.S.C. § 1608 (1958). For the loan of civilian technicians as one phase of its program, the Committee also made use of Public Law 63, approved May 3, 1939 (53 Stat. 652), which authorized the temporary loan of civilian employees of the United States government to provide advice and assistance to the governments of the American republics, as well as to those of Liberia and the Philippines. This Act supplemented provisions of earlier legislation making available the services of military and naval advisers to the American republics.

13. Philip M. Glick, *The Administration of Technical Assistance: Growth in the Americas* (Chicago: University of Chicago Press, 1957), pp. 10–14.

14. The text of Departmental Order No. 367 of July 27, 1938, is given in *Press Releases*, Vol. XIX, No. 461, July 30, 1938 (Washington: Government Printing Office, 1939), p. 66.

15. *Official Trip of Examination of Federal Activities in South and Central America*, House Report of a Subcommittee of the Committee on Appropriations, 77th Cong., 1st sess. (December 4, 1941), p. 27.

16. Other members of the General Advisory Committee at the time were Robert G. Caldwell of the Massachusetts Institute of Technology; Ben M. Cherrington of the University of Denver, previously Chief of the Division of Cultural Relations; Stephen P. Duggan, Director, Institute of International Education; Waldo G. Leland, Director, American Council of Learned Societies; Archibald MacLeish, Librarian of Congress; Carl H. Milam, Secretary, American Library Association; James T. Shotwell, Chairman, National Committee of the United States of America on International Intellectual Cooperation; George N. Shuster, President, Hunter College; and John W. Studebaker, United States Commissioner of Education.

17. Department of State, Division of Cultural Relations, Minutes of General Advisory Committee, September 17–18, 1941 (mimeographed), pp. 34–45.

18. *Congressional Record*, Vol. 87 (April 3, 1941), 3019–20.

19. Minutes of General Advisory Committee, September 17–18, 1941, cited, p. 45.

20. Richard F. Pattee, *Cultural Relations Between the United States and the Other American Republics* (Washington: George Washington University Press, 1939), p. 4. Mr. Pattee was an officer of the Division of Cultural Relations.

21. *Department of State Bulletin*, 1939, 1:492–93.

22. *Department of State Appropriation Bill for 1940*, House hearings, 76th Cong., 2d sess. (1940), p. 32. In 1939 Congress appropriated $75,-000 for the official exchanges under the Buenos Aires Convention. In June, 1940, approximately $70,000 was voted for travel grants to students and a small number of outstanding intellectual leaders.

23. *Department of State Appropriation Bill, 1944*, House hearings, 78th Cong., 2d sess. (1944), p. 203, statement of Under-Secretary of State Sumner Welles.

24. Department of State, Division of Cultural Relations, Minutes of General Advisory Committee, February 23–24, 1943 (mimeographed), p. 9.

25. "Outline of Tentative Program for the Division of Cultural Relations" (Washington: Department of State, June 1, 1939, mimeographed), pp. 1, 2.

26. Minutes of General Advisory Committee, February 23–24, 1943, cited, pp. 17–18.

27. Minutes of General Advisory Committee, June 28–29, 1944, cited, pp. 49–50.

28. Morrill Cody, "The Work of the Cultural Relations Attaché," *Department of State Bulletin*, 1945, 12:574–75; and Howard Lee Nostrand, *The Cultural Attaché* (New Haven, Conn.: Edward W. Hazen Foundation, n.d.).

29. *Science and Foreign Relations* (Washington: Department of State, 1950).

30. These trends are noted in detail in Donald H. Scott, "The Cultural Institute in Mexico City as an Example of the United States Policy in Cultural Relations" (unpublished Ph.D. dissertation, University of Southern California, 1959), pp. 44–55.

31. *Progress Report of the Division of Cultural Relations, Department of State* (Washington, 1940, mimeographed), pp. 13–14.

32. Department of State, Division of Cultural Relations, Minutes of General Advisory Committee, February 25, 1942, pp. 37–38.

33. *Ibid.*, pp. 30–31. See also the Minutes of the meetings of June

19–20, 1942, pp. 23–27; February 23–24, 1943, pp. 22–31; June 19–20, 1943, pp. 18–31; February 18–19, 1944, pp. 7–17; and June 28–29, 1944, pp. 3–33.

34. The Agency was called the "Office for Coordination of Commercial and Cultural Relations between the American Republics" from August 16, 1940, to July 30, 1941; the "Office of the Coordinator of Inter-American Affairs" from July 30, 1941, to March 23, 1945; and the "Office of Inter-American Affairs" from March 23, 1945, to its termination on May 20, 1946.

35. *History of the Office of the Coordinator of Inter-American Affairs* (Washington: Government Printing Office, 1947), p. 7, footnote 15. This source will hereafter in this chapter be cited as *History*.

36. *Ibid.*, p. 266.

37. Charles A. H. Thomson, *Overseas Information Service of the United States Government* (Washington: The Brookings Institution, 1948), pp. 117–21, 147–51.

38. Secretary of State Cordell Hull was fearful that a sharp increase in activities during the war followed by an abrupt abandonment at the close of the conflict, as had happened in World War I, would raise doubts "as to the bona fide character of our real interest." For an expression of this view, see *First Supplemental National Defense Appropriation Bill, 1943*, House hearings, 78th Cong., 1st sess. (1943), p. 564.

39. On the activities of the Institute of Inter-American Affairs, see *History*, cited, pp. 115–36; and of the Inter-American Educational Foundation, *ibid.*, pp. 100–103. Both agencies are also discussed in Glick, cited, pp. 14–30. The two corporations were merged in 1947 by an act of Congress, under the title of the second; and this agency was absorbed into the Technical Cooperation Administration of the Department of State, established to carry out the Act for International Development, which in 1950 authorized the Point Four program of technical assistance.

40. For a fuller discussion of the *servicio* see Glick, cited, pp. 17–22, 68–69, and 296–301.

41. *History*, cited, pp. 105–13.

42. Executive Order of June 13, 1942, *Federal Register* (June 16, 1942), pp. 4468–69. An Executive Order of March 9, 1943, further defined the task of the agency. *Ibid.* (March 12, 1943), p. 3021. The OWI consolidated functions which had previously been carried on by the Office of Facts and Figures, the Office of Government Reports, the Foreign In-

formation Activities of the Coordinator of Information and the war information functions of the Office for Emergency Management.

43. No official history of the Office of War Information has been published. The work of OWI, including its cultural activities, is reviewed in Thomson, cited, pp. 17–92.

44. Richard H. Heindel, "U.S. Libraries Overseas," *Survey Graphic* (May, 1946), pp. 162–65; and by the same author, "The American Library Abroad: A Medium of International Intellectual Exchange," *Library Quarterly*, 1946, 16:93–107. See also Carroll, cited, pp. 133–39.

45. Edward W. Barrett, *Truth is our Weapon* (New York: Funk & Wagnalls, 1953), pp. 40–42.

46. Haldore Hanson, *The Cultural-Cooperation Program, 1938–43* (Washington: Government Printing Office, 1944), pp. 12–16, 19–22.

47. *Ibid.,* pp. 30–31.

CHAPTER THREE—THE COLD WAR: 1945–1953

1. On the work of this agency see George Creel, *How We Advertised America* (New York: Harper, 1920) and James R. Mock and Cedric Larson, *Words That Won the War* (Princeton: Princeton University Press, 1939).

2. The text of the President's statement and of the Executive Order is given in *Department of State Bulletin*, 1945, 13:306–307.

3. Its name had been changed in a reorganization of the Department of State in January, 1944, to that of Division of Science, Education and Art; and again changed in June of that year to that of Division of Cultural Cooperation. The term "exchange of persons" now widely used for the organized two-way travel of students, professors, and other specialized personnel first appeared in 1946 as the title of the new division handling such programs. For its relations to "Exchange" and "Educational exchange" generally, see p. 205, note 31.

4. *Department of State Bulletin*, 1945, 13:589–93. For numerous other statements by government officials during this period emphasizing the aim of "peace through understanding," the important role of private agencies, and the need for a factual, nonpropaganda information program to overcome ignorance, suspicion, and prejudice, see Donald H. Scott,

"The Cultural Institute in Mexico City as an Example of the United States Policy in Cultural Relations" (unpublished Ph.D. dissertation, University of Southern California, 1959), pp. 70–84.

5. Strictly speaking, the Act was the Fulbright amendment to the Surplus Property Act of 1944, as amended. It was Public Law 584, 79th Cong., 1st sess., 60 Stat. 754, approved August 1, 1946. The text as amended is given in *Legislation on Foreign Relations with Explanatory Notes*, Senate, Committee on Foreign Relations, 84th Cong., 2d sess. (1957), pp. 123–24.

6. Data from the Bureau of Educational and Cultural Affairs, Department of State. That these grants constituted almost 75 per cent of all individual grants under the Exchange of Persons Program of the Department of State (66,600) is one indication of the significance of the Act.

7. The membership of the Board through 1956 is given in Department of State, *Swords into Ploughshares* (Washington, 1956).

8. Francis J. Colligan, "U.S. Government Exchange Programs with the Other American Republics," *News Bulletin of the Institute of International Education*, Vol. 30, No. 7 (April, 1955), p. 2.

9. *Foreign Educational Benefits and Surplus Property*, Senate hearings, Committee on Military Affairs, 78th Cong., 1st sess., February 25, 1946, pp. 3–4. For Senator Fulbright's original speech in favor of his proposal, see *Congressional Record*, Vol. 91 (September 27, 1945), p. 9044. In this he declared: "If this bill is approved the funds will be used to exchange students, create a better understanding of our mutual problems, and promote friendly relations. . . ."

10. See pp. 18–19.

11. *Foreign Educational Benefits and Surplus Property*, Senate hearings, cited, pp. 5–6.

12. Senator Fulbright has stated that it was brought up in the Senate at five o'clock in the afternoon when only a handful of Senators were on the floor, and passed by "unanimous consent." Douglass Cater, *World Progress through Educational Exchange: The Story of a Conference* (New York: Institute of International Education, 1959), p. 9.

13. *Foreign Educational Benefits and Surplus Property*, Senate hearings, cited, pp. 31–35.

14. Walter H. C. Laves and Charles A. Thomson, *Unesco: Purpose, Progress, Prospects* (Bloomington: Indiana University Press, 1957), pp. 18–24, 320–24.

15. *United States Information and Educational Exchange Act of 1947*, House hearings on H.R. 3342, 80th Cong., 1st sess. (1947), pp. 21–22, 35, 138, 171–72, 205–206.

16. His original request for $26 million had been reduced by the Bureau of the Budget to $19 million and by the House to $10 million, but was restored by the Senate to almost $20 million.

17. On the House action and reasons therefor, see *State, Justice, and the Judiciary Appropriation Bill, 1948*, House Report No. 336, 80th Cong., 1st sess. (1948), pp. 6–7.

18. *Congressional Record*, Vol. 93 (June 10, 1947), p. 6754.

19. On the Bloom bill (H.R. 4982), see *Interchange of Knowledge and Skills between People of the United States and Peoples of Other Countries*, House hearings, 79th Cong., 1st and 2d sess., 1945; and *Congressional Record*, Vol. 92 (July 20, 1946), pp. 9591–95. On H.R. 3342, which came to be known as the Smith-Mundt Act, see *United States Information and Educational Exchange Act of 1947*, House hearings, cited; *Congressional Record*, Vol. 93 (June 5, 1947), pp. 6490–92; (June 6, 1947), pp. 6538–78; (June 9, 1947), p. 6625; (June 10, 1947), pp. 6740–54; (June 13, 1947), pp. 6962–99; (June 20, 1947), pp. 7499–7520; and (June 24, 1947), pp. 7609–18; *United States Information and Educational Exchange Act of 1947*, Senate hearings; Senate Report No. 573, 80th Cong., 1st sess.; Senate Report No. 811, 80th Cong., 2d sess.; *Congressional Record*, Vol. 94 (January 16, 1948), pp. 243–74. The report of the Smith-Mundt group of Senators and Representatives visiting Europe is given in *The United States Information Service in Europe*, Senate Report No. 855, 80th Cong., 2d sess. (1948), and Appendix.

20. *Departments of State, Justice, Commerce, and the Judiciary Appropriation Bill, 1950*, Senate hearings, 81st Cong., 1st sess. (1950), p. 271.

21. Cater, cited, p. 10.

22. U.S. 62 Stat. 7, Public Law 402, 80th Cong., 2d sess. (1948), 22 U.S.C. § 1446 (1958).

23. *The United States Information Service in Europe*, Senate Report No. 855, cited, pp. 1, 2.

24. Oren Stephens, *Facts to a Candid World* (Stanford, California: Stanford University Press, 1955), p. 38.

25. *The United States Information Service in Europe*, Senate Report No. 855, cited, pp. 1, 6; and Charles A. H. Thomson, *Overseas Informa-*

tion Service of the United States Government (Washington: The Brookings Institution, 1948), p. 297. Senator Smith in Senate Report No. 855, p. 11 went so far in the direction of psychological warfare as to say, "The Voice of America should, with the aim of discomforting the local government and encouraging the resistance of the people in totalitarian and satellite countries, broadcast back to the country concerned news items and commentaries on events, the publicity of which the local authorities seek to suppress."

26. *Cultural Relations between the United States and the Soviet Union,* State Department Publication No. 3480, International Information and Cultural Series No. 4 (Washington, 1949).

27. *United States Information and Educational Exchange Act of 1947,* Senate hearings, cited, p. 111, testimony of William Benton. The first government propaganda effort to use foreign-language broadcasts to other peoples took place in 1936, when the Nazi government of Germany initiated a Russian-language program to go over the heads of the Soviet government and reach its people. Shortly afterward the Nazis instituted programs in English and French. In 1938 the British and French networks started official programs in foreign languages. The United States began such activities only in 1942, after Pearl Harbor. From 1929, CBS and NBC had carried on short-wave broadcasts as a commercial venture in Spanish to Latin America, but had received no government support. With World War II, the private enterprises could no longer draw revenue from advertising for their foreign-language programs. At their suggestion the government through CIAA and OWI took over the activity for the duration of the conflict. George V. Allen, "The Voice of America," *Department of State Bulletin,* 1948, 19:568.

28. No attempt had earlier been made in committee hearings to draw a distinction between cultural activities and information. Nor did the question come up in the House floor debate except for a single reference by Congressman J. Edgar Chenoweth of Colorado. *Congressional Record,* Vol. 93 (June 6, 1947), p. 6543.

29. Charles A. Thomson succeeded him and was succeeded in 1944 by Bryn Hovde.

30. On the above section, see *Congressional Record,* Vol. 93 (June 6, 1947), p. 6543; *ibid.,* Vol. 94 (January 16, 1948), p. 248; *The United States Information Service in Europe,* Senate Report No. 855, cited, p. 6;

and Ben M. Cherrington, "Ten Years After," *Association of American Colleges Bulletin*, Vol. XXXIV, No. 4 (December, 1948), pp. 509, 514, 522.

31. *The United States Information Service in Europe*, Senate Report No. 855, cited, p. 6; and *United States Information and Educational Exchange Act of 1947*, Senate Report No. 811, cited, p. 11.

32. In 1949, France, Great Britain, and the United States agreed to establish a central government for West Germany, and approved an Occupation Statute. The three Western zones of occupation were fused. The Office of Military Government of the United States for Germany (OMGUS) was replaced by the Office of the U.S. High Commissioner for Germany (HICOG), with authority in Washington transferred from the Department of the Army to the Department of State. OMGUS was primarily a military organization, HICOG essentially a civilian one. Following 1949, U.S. cultural and information activities were extended throughout what had formerly been the three Western zones.

33. On the work of the Commission for International Educational Reconstruction see Harold E. Snyder, *When Peoples Speak to Peoples* (Washington: American Council on Education, 1953), pp. 32–57; and for that of the Commission on Occupied Areas see Harold E. Snyder and George E. Beauchamp, *An Experiment in International Cultural Relations: A Report of the Staff of the Commission on the Occupied Areas* (Washington: American Council on Education, 1951).

34. For the early objectives in Germany see Thomson, cited, pp. 241–42, 255–57. For a summary of education policy concerning Japan see "The Program for Reeducation in Japan: A Survey of Policy," Department of State, *Documents & State Papers*, 1948, 1:3–31. A realistic picture of how education policy was actually formulated is given in Robert King Hall, *Education for a New Japan* (New Haven: Yale University Press, 1949), pp. 69–84. A sober and comprehensive review of the Japanese Occupation is provided by a Dutch official in Baron E. J. Lewe Van Aduard, *Japan: From Surrender to Peace* (The Hague: Martinus Nijhoff, 1953).

35. William Ernest Hocking, *Experiment in Education: What We Can Learn from Teaching Germany* (Chicago: Regnery, 1954), p. 128.

36. United States activities affecting German education are reviewed in Harold Zink, *The United States in Germany, 1944–1955* (New York: Van Nostrand, 1957), pp. 193–214.

37. George N. Shuster, "The American Occupation and German Education," *Proceedings of the American Philosophical Society,* 1953, 97:161.

38. *Departments of State and Justice, the Judiciary, and Related Agencies Appropriations,* 1956, Senate hearings on H.R. 5502, 84th Cong., 1st sess., February 18, 1955, p. 21.

39. Zink, cited, pp. 215–33.

40. *Ibid.,* pp. 234–50.

41. In addition to the article in *Documents & State Papers,* the educational activities of the Occupation are reviewed in Supreme Commander for the Allied Powers, General Headquarters, Civil Information and Education Section, "Mission and Accomplishments of the Occupation in the Civil Information and Education Fields" (Washington, January 1, 1950). The accomplishments of the Occupation are analyzed in Robert S. Schwantes, *Japanese and Americans: A Century of Cultural Relations* (New York: Harper, 1955), pp. 121–28. For a balanced review by a Japanese author (formerly a newspaper editor in Tokyo) of the educational efforts of the Occupation, in which criticism is tempered by a consistent tendency to give the Occupation the benefit of the doubt, see Kazuo Kawai, *Japan's American Interlude* (Chicago: University of Chicago Press, 1960), pp. 183–224.

42. Schwantes, cited, pp. 128, 145.

43. Supreme Commander for the Allied Powers, Civil Information and Education Section, *Post-War Developments in Japanese Education,* Vol. I (Tokyo, 1952), pp. 376–94; Schwantes, cited, pp. 174–75, 197–98; and John W. Bennett, Herbert Passin, and Robert K. McKnight, *In Search of Identity: The Japanese Overseas Scholar in America and Japan* (Minneapolis: University of Minnesota Press, 1958), pp. 47, 101.

44. *Post-War Developments in Japanese Education,* Vol. I, cited, pp. 369–71. Schwantes, cited, pp. 308–11 presents a picture in some detail of the work of the center at Kobe.

45. Schwantes, cited, pp. 226–28, 240, 244.

46. *Congressional Record,* Vol. 96 (March 22, 1950), p. 3764. While Communist doctrine is more specific on the role of propaganda in internal affairs, propaganda has also been recognized as an integral element in Soviet foreign policy. No important move is undertaken without consideration of its psychological impact. Conversely, propaganda prepares for

and follows up political strategy and tactics. In the Soviet view, world opinion is sufficiently significant to warrant prodigious effort to make it an ally rather than an enemy in the struggle with the United States and the other nations of the West. Council on Foreign Relations, *The United States in World Affairs, 1952* (New York: Harper & Brothers, 1952), pp. 29–30. A brief analysis of the development of the Communist concept of propaganda is given in Evron M. Kirkpatrick, ed., *Target: The World: Communist Propaganda Activities in 1955* (New York: Macmillan, 1956). For fuller discussions of Soviet theory on propaganda, see Alex Inkeles, *Public Opinion in Soviet Russia* (Cambridge, Mass.: Harvard University Press, 1950); and Nathan C. Leites, *A Study of Bolshevism* (Glencoe, Ill.: Free Press, 1953), Chapter XV, "Propaganda."

47. The five original members of the Advisory Commission on Educational Exchange were Harvie Branscomb, Chancellor of Vanderbilt University, Chairman; Mark Starr, Educational Director, International Ladies Garment Workers Union, Vice-Chairman; Karl Taylor Compton, President of the Massachusetts Institute of Technology; Harold Willis Dodds, President of Princeton University; and Martin R. P. McGuire, Dean, Catholic University of America. For subsequent members and for the membership of the Advisory Commission on Information, see periodical reports of the Commissions.

48. He said, "We must make ourselves known as we really are—not as Communist propaganda pictures us. We must pool our efforts with those of the other free peoples in a sustained, intensified program to promote the cause of freedom against the propaganda of slavery. We must make ourselves heard round the world in a great campaign of truth." Harry S. Truman, "Fight False Propaganda with Truth," *Department of State Bulletin,* 1950, 22:669–72, particularly p. 672.

49. *Congressional Record,* Vol. 96 (March 22, 1950), pp. 3765–66, Senate Resolution No. 243. Mr. Benton had earlier urged in the meeting of the Executive Committee of the United States National Commission for Unesco in November, 1949, the expansion of the Unesco program and budget to achieve "objectives which are also the objectives of U.S. foreign policy." When subsequently opposition was expressed to the employment of Unesco as an instrument of U.S. foreign policy, Mr. Benton stated that his purpose was not to make the organization an instrument but rather "an ally, an adjunct, an assistance to our foreign policy." United

States National Commission for Unesco, Executive Committee, Summary Minutes of Twelfth Meeting, November 14–15, 1949, p. 13; and Summary Minutes of Thirteenth Meeting, January 30–31, 1950, p. 8.

50. *Sixth Semiannual Report of the Secretary of State to Congress on the International Information and Educational Exchange Program, July 1 to December 31, 1950,* "Launching the Campaign of Truth, First Phase" (Washington, 1951), p. 1.

51. In that area from 1945 to 1949 the number enrolled in various Soviet-oriented cultural societies had mounted from 3,700 to more than 1.3 million. Russian books in translation had been widely distributed. Marxism, Soviet history, and the Russian language were taught in the schools. Hundreds of intellectual, industrial, and political leaders from North Korea visited Moscow for indoctrination, as well as several hundred students. Soviet artists, writers, and other cultural leaders gave nearly 70,-000 lectures and concerts during 1948, and large numbers of Soviet films were shown. *Fifth Semiannual Report on Educational Exchange Activities,* House Doc. No. 108, 82d Cong., 1st sess. (1951), pp. 2, 13–15.

52. Edward W. Barrett, *Truth is Our Weapon* (New York: Funk & Wagnalls, 1953), pp. 78–79.

53. *Sixth Semiannual Report of United States Advisory Commission on Information,* House Doc. No. 526, 82d Cong., 2d sess. (1952), pp. 9–11. A six-fold classification of countries distinguished the Soviet Union and its satellites, crucial countries under threat of aggression, danger zones, vulnerable, sensitive, and noncritical countries. Among new methods employed was the enlistment of indigenous support in foreign countries through the sponsorship by private organizations of leaflets, books, and posters exposing the claims and character of Communist imperialism and upholding the superiority of the free world. Another new technique in the press program involved the use of ambiguous cover designs on leaflets and pamphlets, "calculated to lure pro- as well as anti-Communist readers into sampling the contents." At Rome "one USIS leaflet was so successful that several Communist units were duped into distributing copies to factory workers who were members of the Communist-led unions." *Fifth Semiannual Report of the Secretary of State to Congress on the International Information and Educational Exchange Program, January 1 to June 30, 1950,* p. 2; and *Eighth Semiannual Report . . . July 1 to December 31, 1951,* "Waging the Truth Campaign," p. 1. (Washington, 1951 and 1952 respectively).

54. *Sixth Semiannual Report of United States Advisory Commission on Information,* cited, p. 2.

55. Scott, cited, pp. 105–10.

56. *Third Semiannual Report on Educational Exchange Activities,* House Doc. No. 556, 81st Cong., 2d sess. (1950), p. 6.

57. *Third Semiannual Report on Educational Exchange Activities,* cited, pp. 6–7.

58. *Sixth Semiannual Report on Educational Exchange Activities,* House Doc. No. 321, 82d Cong., 2d sess. (1952), p. 1.

59. *Third Semiannual Report on Educational Exchange Activities,* cited, p. 6.

60. *Fifth Semiannual Report on Educational Exchange Activities,* cited, p. 3.

61. *Overseas Information Programs of the United States,* Senate hearings, Part 2, Committee on Foreign Relations, 83d Cong., 1st sess. (1953), pp. 1027, 1450–51.

62. *Fifth Semiannual Report on Educational Exchange Activities,* cited, p. 3.

63. Dan Lacy, "Aid to National Policy," *Library Trends,* 1953, 2:146–70.

64. *Eighth Semiannual Report on Educational Exchange Activities,* House Doc. No. 35, 83d Cong., 1st sess. (1953), p. 4.

65. *Supplemental Appropriation Bill for 1951,* House hearings, p. 5; *Departments of State, Justice, Commerce, and the Judiciary Appropriations,* 1952, Senate hearings, 82d Cong., 1st sess. (1952), Part 2, p. 1786; and *Fifth Semiannual Report on Educational Exchange Activities,* cited, p. 3.

66. The use of students as propaganda agents had apparently been a matter of controversy in the Department of State, between the proponents of information and those of educational exchange. One official reported in 1952 that it had been discussed, as regards both foreign students returning from the United States and American students going abroad. Another declared that student exchanges were an excellent means of propaganda in the broad sense, but no attempt was made to "indoctrinate." *Overseas Information Programs of the United States,* Senate hearings, Part 1, 1952, cited, pp. 112, 195–96.

67. Scott, cited, pp. 110–16. For discussion of these questions in the immediate postwar period, see Thomson, cited, pp. 308–309, 327–29.

68. For the story of this incident see Philip M. Glick, *The Administration of Technical Assistance: Growth in the Americas* (Chicago: University of Chicago Press, 1957), pp. 30–31; and Jonathan B. Bingham, *Shirt-Sleeve Diplomacy: Point 4 in Action* (New York: John Day Co., 1953), pp. 10, 268. Mr. Hardy was later named director of information for the Technical Cooperation Administration and lost his life in an airplane crash, together with the administrator of the agency, Dr. Henry G. Bennett. On that occasion both President Truman and Secretary of State Acheson gave Hardy public credit as the originator of the Point Four idea.

69. The President spoke of four courses of action to be emphasized by the United States in its international relations. The first three were: to continue support of the United Nations and related agencies; to continue programs for world economic recovery; and to strengthen freedom-loving nations against the dangers of aggression. Point Four outlined a "bold new program for making the benefits of our scientific advances and industrial progress available for the improvement and growth of under-developed areas."

70. "Inaugural Address of the President," *Department of State Bulletin*, 1949, 20:125.

71. Bingham, cited, p. 12.

72. Public Law 535, 81st Cong., 2d sess., 64 Stat. 198 (1950). For a summary of the purpose, scope, and execution of the proposed program, see Department of State, *Point Four* (Washington, 1950, Pub. 3719).

73. The prompt expansion of technical and economic assistance was recommended by two official reports, Gordon Gray's *Report to the President on Foreign Economic Policies* (Washington: Government Printing Office, 1950); and *Partners in Progress: A Report to the President by the International Development Advisory Board* (under the chairmanship of Nelson A. Rockefeller) (Washington: Government Printing Office, 1951).

74. *Overseas Information Programs of the United States*, Senate hearings, Part 1, cited, pp. 215–26.

75. *Ibid.*, p. 86; and *Overseas Information Programs of the United States*, Senate Report No. 406, 83d Cong., 1st sess. (1953), pp. 58, 139–40.

76. *Overseas Information Programs of the United States*, Senate hearings, cited, pp. 79–95.

77. Lincoln Gordon, "The Development of United States Representation Overseas," in *The Representation of the United States Abroad,* cited, p. 34.

78. *Overseas Information Programs of the United States,* Senate hearings, Part 1, cited, pp. 22–35; *Government Programs in International Education,* cited, pp. 78–85; and Institute of International Education, *Report of Community Hospitality Workshop-Leader Programs,* Third National Conference on Exchange of Persons (Washington, 1959, mimeographed), p. 2.

CHAPTER FOUR—EXPANSION: 1953–1962

1. Dan Lacy, "Aid to National Policy," *Library Trends,* 1953, 2:165–66.

2. Its title was the Select Committee of the Senate on Overseas Information Programs. It met in accordance with the terms of the Benton resolution already mentioned (p. 79), which as reintroduced in a modified version in February, 1951, had urged a comprehensive study of the international information programs of the United States government. *Congressional Record,* Vol. 97 (February 19, 1951), pp. 1355–59.

3. For the hearings, which totaled almost 1,900 pages, see *Overseas Information Programs of the United States,* Subcommittee of the Senate Committee on Foreign Relations, 83d Cong., 1st sess. (1953), Parts 1 and 2. The findings of the committee are given in *Overseas Information Programs of the United States,* Senate Report No. 406, 83d Cong., 1st sess. (1953); and Senate Report No. 936, 83d Cong., 2d sess. (1954). The staff studies are included in the first of these two reports.

4. *Overseas Information Programs of the United States,* Senate Report No. 406, cited, pp. 22–33.

5. As Assistant Secretary of State: William Benton, 1945–47; George V. Allen, 1948–50; Edward W. Barrett, 1950–52; as administrator, International Information Administration: Wilson Compton, 1952–53; and Robert L. Johnson, 1953.

6. *Department of State Bulletin,* 1953, 28:210.

7. *Ibid.,* 1953, 28:217.

8. *Ibid.,* 1953, 29:125–26.

9. *State Department Information Program—Information Centers,* Senate hearings, 82d Cong., 2d sess. (1953), Part 1, pp. 44, 48. At the time of the Budenz charge, the overseas libraries contained among their 100,000 titles by 85,000 authors thirty-nine copies of works by eight authors publicly known as affiliated with the Communist cause. The authors were Earl Browder, Ilya Ehrenberg, William Z. Foster, Maxim Gorki, Trofim D. Lysenko, John Reed, Agnes Smedley, and Anna Louise Strong. For a list of the thirty-nine copies, see *Supplemental Appropriation Bill,* House hearings, 83d Cong., 1st sess. (1954), Part 1, pp. 593–94. These copies had apparently been inherited from earlier libraries taken over or had been acquired locally, rather than purchased with appropriated funds.

10. The text of this and subsequent directives cited is given in *Overseas Information Programs of the United States,* Senate hearings, Part 3, cited, pp. 1600–22. A brief collection of writings presenting various facets of the question is given in Walter M. Daniels, ed., *The Censorship of Books* (The Reference Shelf, Vol. 26, No. 5) (New York: H. W. Wilson, 1954), pp. 107–20.

11. *The United States Information Service in Europe,* Senate Report No. 855, 80th Cong., 2d sess. (1948), pp. 13–14.

12. On March 7, 1952, a supplementary directive gave particular attention to the books of Howard Fast. It laid down as a general principle that "the facilities of the United States Information Service are not available under any circumstances for encouraging, facilitating, or promoting the study of, or interest in, communism for any purpose at any time." It noted that while some of Mr. Fast's books "support a Communist line," others such as a study of Thomas Paine "vividly portray certain traditional American freedoms which are denied in all Communist countries." It therefore ordered removal of volumes of the first type and authorized "judicious use" of those of the second type when they might "achieve an effective propaganda result with readers having some Communist leanings by taking advantage of the credence given them by favorable Communist comment, especially their support of certain human rights and individual liberties."

13. Its members appointed in 1952 by the Secretary of State were: Martin R. P. McGuire, professor, Catholic University (chairman);

George P. Brett, president, the Macmillan Co.; Cass Canfield, chairman of the board, Harper & Bros.; Robert L. Crowell, president, Thomas Y. Crowell Co.; Robert B. Downs, director of libraries, University of Illinois; Morris Hadley, president, New York Public Library; Lewis Hanke, director, Institute of Latin American Studies, University of Texas; and Keyes D. Metcalf, director of libraries, Harvard University.

14. *Eighth Semiannual Report on Educational Exchange Activities,* House Doc. No. 35, 83d Cong., 1st sess. (1953), pp. 5–6.

15. *Ninth Semiannual Report on Educational Exchange Activities,* House Doc. No. 154, 83d Cong., 1st sess. (1953), pp. 23–24.

16. *Overseas Information Programs of the United States,* Senate hearings, Part 2, cited, pp. 388–90.

17. Robert L. Crowell, President of Thomas Y. Crowell Co., a private publisher who had served as consultant on principles of book selection to the Department of State, testified concerning past policy on March 9, 1953, "more often is a book vetoed when it should not be than accepted when it should not be." *Ibid.,* p. 311.

18. Removed from some of the libraries, in addition to works by known Communists, were books by Bert Andrews of the *New York Herald Tribune;* Whittaker Chambers, leading witness against Alger Hiss; Foster Rhea Dulles, cousin of the Secretary of State; Clarence Streit, proponent of North Atlantic Union; and Walter White of the National Association for the Advancement of Colored People. Martin Merson, *The Private Diary of a Public Servant* (New York: Macmillan, 1955), pp. 13–15. Mr. Merson was executive officer to Dr. Robert L. Johnson, Administrator of the International Information Administration from March through July, 1953.

19. *Tenth Semiannual Report on Educational Exchange Activities,* House Doc. No. 294, 83d Cong., 2d sess. (1954), p. 27.

20. *The New York Times,* June 15, 1953, p. 10.

21. The statement was originally prepared by a group of librarians, publishers, and others which met in May under the chairmanship of Luther H. Evans, then Librarian of Congress. In addition to the American Library Association, it was officially approved by the American Book Publishers Council, the American Booksellers Association, the Defense Commission of the National Education Association, and other national organizations. A vigorous statement of similar tenor was adopted by the American Bar Association in August.

22. American Library Association, *ALA Bulletin*, 1953, 47:481–83, 487.

23. In contrast to his claim that 30,000 publications by Communist authors were on the library shelves, investigation eventually revealed the presence of approximately 2,000 volumes written (aside from the eight known Communists who are listed in note 9, p. 212) by some thirty alleged pro-Communists. These volumes were ordered off the shelves. *Supplemental Appropriation Bill*, 1954, Senate hearings, 83d Cong., 1st sess. (1954), pp. 25, 656.

24. U.S. Information Agency, *First Review of Operations*, August–December, 1953 (Washington, 1954), p. 8.

25. *Ibid.*, p. 8.

26. Supplemental Appropriations for Fiscal Year 1954, Senate, Committee on Appropriations, 83d Cong., 1st sess. (1953), p. 615.

27. On the establishment of the new agency see "International Information Administration Established," *Department of State Bulletin*, 1952, 26:151; and *Sixth Semiannual Report of United States Advisory Commission on Information*, House Doc. No. 526, 82d Cong., 2d sess. (1952), pp. 20–24. On the question of title see *Seventh Semiannual Report on Educational Exchange Activities*, House Doc. No. 412, 82d Cong., 2d sess. (1952), p. iv. It was later stated that the title of the new agency was abbreviated on the assumption that information encompassed education. However, the head of the agency ordered all its letterheads to carry at the bottom of the sheet the phrase, "International Information and Educational Exchange Program." *Overseas Information Programs of the United States*, Senate hearings, Part 1, cited, pp. 198–99.

28. *Seventh Semiannual Report of United States Advisory Commission on Information*, House Doc. No. 94, 83d Cong., 1st sess. (1953), pp. 1–7.

29. See *Reorganization Plans Nos. 7 and 8 of 1953*, House hearings, Committee on Government Operations, 82d Cong., 2d sess. (June 22–24, 1953), p. 161. The hearings set forth in considerable detail the arguments for a separate agency. Reorganization Plan No. 7 had to do with foreign aid and the establishment of the Foreign Operations Administration. Dr. Johnson, the last administrator of the IIA, was succeeded by the Messrs. Theodore Streibert, Arthur Larson, Ambassador George V. Allen, and Edward R. Murrow as directors of the United States Information Agency.

30. *Department of State Bulletin,* 1953, 29:756.

31. *Overseas Information Programs of the United States,* Senate hearings, Part 2, cited, pp. 863, 1046.

32. *Ibid.,* pp. 863–64, 898–99.

33. Senator Mundt contemplated for a time amending the Smith-Mundt Act by a requirement that the educational exchange service be administered separately from information activities. *Congressional Record,* Vol. 99 (April 30, 1953), p. 4205 (Senate Doc. No. 1802, 83d Cong., 1st sess.).

34. *Overseas Information Programs of the United States,* Senate Report No. 406, cited, p. 24.

35. *Tenth Semiannual Report on Educational Exchange Activities,* cited, pp. 8–9.

36. See p. 90.

37. See p. 116.

38. *U.S. Information Agency Instruction No. CA-8 of July 6, 1954* (Washington, 1954). USIA in 1956 set up a Cultural Operations Division, and broadened the title of its Advisory Committee on Books Abroad to that of Advisory Committee on Cultural Information.

39. Department of State, memorandum of January 4, 1955, entitled "Principles to be Observed in Administering the Educational Exchange Program and the Overseas Information Program (Washington, 1955)," from Undersecretary of State Robert Murphy to Assistant Secretary of State Carl W. McCardle. It carried among several attachments a memorandum on "Clarification of Distinction Between Cultural Activities of USIA and Educational Exchange Activities of the Department."

40. *Report of the State-USIA Task Force on International Cultural Activities* (Washington, April 22, 1955).

41. *Fourteenth Report of the United States Advisory Commission on Information,* House Doc. No. 106, 86th Cong., 1st sess. (1959), pp. 8–11.

42. Statements of George V. Allen, Director of the United States Information Agency, and Saxton Bradford, Deputy Director, in respectively, *Tenth Review of Operations,* January 1—June 30, 1958, p. 3; and *The Annapolis Conference on International Education,* April 4–5, 1959 (Washington: Department of State, Bureau of International Cultural Relations, July 27, 1959), pp. 13–15.

43. J. L. Morrill, *A Proposal for the Coordination of the Exchange of*

Persons Programs of the International Educational Exchange Service and of the International Cooperation Administration, Part II (Washington: Department of State, May 1, 1956, mimeographed), p. 5. Hereafter this source will be cited as *Morrill Report*. The ICA figures did not include administrative costs or costs of foreign nationals employed on technical cooperation projects.

44. *Conference Report on Departments of State and Justice, the Judiciary, and Related Agencies Appropriations Bill, 1956*, House Report No. 1043, 84th Cong., 1st sess. (1956); and *Morrill Report*, Part II, cited, pp. 1–5.

45. Section 302 of the Mutual Security Act of 1954 defined technical cooperation as follows: ". . . the term 'technical cooperation programs' means programs for the international exchange of technical knowledge and skills designed to contribute to the balanced and integrated development of the economic resources and productive capacities of economically under-developed areas." *Morrill Report*, cited, Part V, p. 35.

46. *Ibid.*, Part V, pp. 36–38, 40.

47. *Ibid.*, Part I, p. 1.

48. *Ibid.*, Part IV, p. 22, and Part V, p. 42 (italics added). For the complete text of the statement, see "U.S. Government Participation in Cultural Exchange Programs," *Looking Ahead*, Vol. 4, No. 3 (Washington: National Planning Association, April, 1956), pp. 5–8.

49. Andrew Berding, *Foreign Affairs and You* (New York: Doubleday, 1962), p. 212.

49a. *Toward a National Effort in International Educational and Cultural Affairs, Twenty-Sixth Semi-Annual Report on Educational Exchange Activities*, 87th Cong., 1st sess., House Doc. No. 199, Committee on Foreign Affairs (Washington: Government Printing Office, 1961). Also available as Department of State Publication No. 7238 (July 1961).

50. The Bureau, established July 2, 1959, comprises the Office of Educational Exchange (OEE), formerly the International Educational Exchange Service; and the Office of Cultural Exchange (OCE), which includes what was formerly the Cultural Presentations Staff for the President's Program in the Arts, the Program Development Staff, and the Unesco Relations Staff.

51. The program for World War II veterans under the Servicemen's Readjustment Act of 1944 (P.L. 346, 78th Cong., 2d sess., 58 Stat. 284 [1944]), terminated substantially in 1956. That for Korean veterans under the Veterans Readjustment Assistance Act of 1952 (P.L. 550, 82d

Cong., 2d sess., 66 Stat. 663 [1952]) was scheduled to end in 1965.

52. For a special review of the Finnish program see Department of State, *An Investment in Understanding: Educational Exchange Program between the United States and Finland, 1950–54* (Washington, 1956). On aid to Chinese students see *Federal Activity in the Field of Education,* House, hearings, Committee on Education and Labor, 83d Cong., 1st sess. (1954), pp. 198–99; Department of State, *The Program of Emergency Aid to Chinese Students, 1949–1955* (Washington, 1956); and Committee on Educational Interchange Policy, *Chinese Students in the United States, 1948–55: A Study in Government Policy* (New York: Institute of International Education, 1956).

53. *Departments of State and Justice, the Judiciary, and Related Agencies Appropriations for 1961: United States Information Agency, President's Special International Program, Commission on Civil Rights,* House hearings, 86th Cong., 2d sess., pp. 813–21. Books constitute 54 per cent of the material exported under the program, periodicals 20 per cent, and motion pictures, 23 per cent. *Ibid.,* p. 889.

54. *Report on the Operations of the Department of State* (under P.L. 584), 86th Cong., 2d sess. (June 3, 1960), House Doc. No. 410, p. 1. For a general summary of the Fulbright program to 1960 and accomplishments of grantees, see Francis J. Colligan, "The Fulbright Act and Grants," *Dictionary of American History,* Vol. VI (New York: Charles Scribner's Sons, 1961), p. 126.

55. *Departments of State, Justice, and Commerce, and the United States Information Agency Appropriations, 1955,* Senate hearings, 83d Cong., 1st sess., Part 2, pp. 1172–1201, 1769–1845.

56. *Departments of State, Justice, the Judiciary, and Related Agencies Appropriations, 1956,* Senate hearings, cited, pp. 165–254.

57. *Congressional Record,* Vol. 101 (April 14, 1955), pp. 4460–4499.

58. *Fifteenth Semiannual Report on Educational Exchange Activities,* House Doc. No. 335, 84th Cong., 2d sess. (1956), pp. 1–3.

59. *United States Information and Educational Exchange Act Amendments of 1956,* Senate hearings, pp. 104–105; and *Departments of State, Justice, the Judiciary, and Related Agencies Appropriations, 1957,* Senate hearings, 84th Cong., 2d sess., pp. 441–442.

60. *1956 Amendments to the United States Information and Educational Exchange Act of 1948,* Senate Report No. 1959, 84th Cong., 2d sess. (1956), p. 7.

61. *Departments of State, Justice, the Judiciary, and Related Agencies Appropriations, 1959,* Senate hearings, 86th Cong., 1st sess., pp. 16, 24.

62. Francis A. Young, "Educational and Cultural Exchange, the Fulbright-Hays Act of 1961," *American Council of Learned Societies Newsletter,* Vol. XII, No. 9 (November, 1961), pp. 3–7.

63. *Ibid.*

64. Ralph Purcell, *Government and Art* (Washington: Public Affairs Press, 1956), pp. 84, 85.

65. *Federal Grants for Fine Arts Programs and Projects,* House, Report of a Special Subcommittee to the Committee on Education and Labor, Committee Print, 83d Cong., 2d sess. (1954), p. 7.

66. Quoted from a newspaper in Djakarta, Indonesia, in House hearings, . . . *for cultural and athletic exchanges and participation in international fairs and festivals,* Committee on Foreign Affairs, 84th Cong., 2d sess. (March 6, 7, 13, and 15, 1956), p. 5.

67. *The President's Emergency Fund for Participation in International Affairs, Supplemental Appropriations Act, 1955,* P.L. 663, 83d Cong., 2d sess., 68 **Stat.** 800, 824 (1954); $2.25 million was allotted to the Department of State for cultural presentations, $2.25 million to the Department of Commerce for trade fairs, and $500,000 to the United States Information Agency for coordination, promotion, and publicity.

68. The sources for the above and the following material are, for the period from December, 1954, to June 30, 1956, the mimeographed *Quarterly Reports* issued by the United States Information Agency under the title "President's Emergency Fund for Participation in International Affairs"; and from July 1, 1956, onward, the successive *Semiannual Reports* issued by USIA entitled "President's Special International Program."

69. *The International Cultural Relations of the United States, Policies and Programs, 1955–1958* (Washington: Department of State, n.d.), pp. 31–33, which summarizes material presented in the Smithsonian Institution; *Report on the National Collection of Fine Arts including the Freer Gallery of Art* (Washington: Government Printing Office, annual). This is an interesting example of international cultural activities of other agencies of the federal government independent of the principal agencies in this field. There are others whose implications for our international relations vary with their terms of reference. Most are listed in Francis J. Colligan, *Programs of International Cultural Cooperation and*

Technical Exchange of Agencies of the U.S. Government and Related International Organizations (Washington, 1957, mimeographed).

70. *Departments of State and Justice, the Judiciary, and Related Agencies Appropriations, 1956,* Senate hearings, cited, pp. 246–47; and *ibid.,* 1957, Senate hearings, cited, p. 643.

71. Columbia-Harvard Research Group under the administration of Columbia University, *United States Foreign Policy, U.S.S.R. and Eastern Europe,* Senate, Committee on Foreign Relations, Committee Print, Study No. 11 (February 14, 1960), p. 32.

72. Department of State, *Report on Exchanges with the Soviet Union and Eastern Europe,* Report No. 18 (January 1, 1962).

73. L. D. Mallory, "A Footnote to Recent History," *Foreign Service Journal,* Vol. 38, No. 3 (March, 1961), pp. 24–25. The text of the Act of Bogota is given in Department of State Bulletin, 1960, 43:537–40.

73a. For a fuller discussion of the issues raised here see Chapter Six and Laves Report, *op. cit.*

74. See *An Act for International Development: Summary Presentation,* Department of State publication 7205, General Foreign Policy Series (Washington, 1961).

75. See, for example, his message to Congress requesting funds for the Alliance, March 14, 1962. For the relation of the Alliance to American foreign policy, past and present, see Milton Eisenhower, "The Alliance for Progress, Historic Roots" in John C. Dreier, ed., *The Alliance for Progress, Problems and Perspectives* (Baltimore: Johns Hopkins Press, 1962), and Dean Rusk, "The Alliance in the Context of World Affairs," *ibid.,* p. 102.

76. See Agency for International Development, *Proposed Program for Fiscal Year 1963,* pp. 3–6 (mimeographed).

77. *Department of State Bulletin,* 1956, 34:919. Late in 1955 Theodore Streibert, then Director of USIA, had discussed with President Eisenhower the agency's need for an enlarged appropriation. The President concurred, but suggested in addition stimulating private groups and individuals to share the task of improving relations with other peoples. He cited what private initiative had achieved in the economic field. American Council on Education, Minutes of the Commission on Education and International Affairs (Washington: November 8–9, 1956, mimeographed), p. 3, statement of Conger Reynolds, Chief, USIA's Office of Private Cooperation.

78. *People to People: A Program of International Friendship* (Washington: United States Information Agency, n.d.).

79. William Harlan Hale, "Every Man an Ambassador," *The Reporter* (March 21, 1957), p. 21.

80. In fiscal year 1961, $10 million was appropriated by Congress for the first year of the Center's operation. An additional $3.3 million was appropriated in fiscal year 1962, for a total of $13.3 million for the two years. For fiscal year 1963 a request was made for $8,343,000. See *Second Annual Report, Center for Cultural and Technical Interchange Between East and West*, University of Hawaii (August 31, 1962, mimeographed).

81. Peace Corps, *First Annual Report to Congress* (Washington, 1962).

82. Some of the principal inquiries are:

The University and World Affairs, a report by a distinguished committee sponsored by the Ford Foundation, J. L. Morrill, Chairman; John B. Howard, Study Director. 1960. Available from Ford Foundation.

Toward a National Effort in International Educational and Cultural Affairs, a report prepared for the United States Advisory Commission on Educational Exchange, Department of State, by Walter H. C. Laves. 1961. Available from Superintendent of Documents, U.S. Government Printing Office. 87th Cong., 1st sess., House Committee on Foreign Affairs, Doc. No. 199.

Report of the President's Committee on Information Activities Abroad, appointed by President Eisenhower; Mansfield Sprague, Chairman; Waldemar A. Neilsen, Executive Director (summarized in *Department of State Bulletin*, February 6, 1961).

The College and University in International Affairs, 1959–60. Annual report of the Carnegie Foundation for the Advancement of Teaching, New York.

Report on Exchange of Persons, by an *ad hoc* task force appointed by President-elect Kennedy; James M. Davis, Chairman. 1961.

A Report to the President of the United States, transmitted by Kenneth Holland, President of the Institute for International Education. 1960.

See also Robert Blum, ed., *Cultural Affairs and Foreign Relations*, The American Assembly, Columbia University (New York: Prentice-Hall, 1963), p. 184.

CHAPTER SIX—CULTURAL RELATIONS AND
FOREIGN POLICY OBJECTIVES

1. OECD, *Policy Conference on Economic Growth and Investment in Education* (Washington, 1962), p. 4.

2. F. Barghoorn, "Soviet Cultural Diplomacy Since Stalin," *The Russian Review,* Vol. 17 (1958), pp. 50–52.

3. The Soviet government for many years has refused membership in certain specialized agencies, such as FAO and the World Bank, and it joined Unesco only in 1954.

4. USIA, *Seventeenth Report to Congress* (Washington, 1962), p. 17.

5. See the stimulating appraisal by former Senator William Benton, "Should We Continue the Cultural Exchanges with the U.S.S.R.?" *Saturday Review* (October 27, 1962), p. 17 ff.

6. USIA, Office Report of Commercial Traffic Section (Washington, March, 1962, mimeographed).

CHAPTER SEVEN—TOWARD AN EFFECTIVE
CULTURAL PROGRAM

1. A partial solution may soon be achieved through the creation of a new private agency stimulated by the Ford Foundation report "The University and World Affairs" (New York, 1960).

2. Probably the most complete discussion of these issues is found in Edward W. Weidner, *The World Role of Universities* (New York, 1962). See here also references to other published studies in the series sponsored by Michigan State University.

Index